T0166575

The Assembled Parties

The
Assembled
Parties

Richard Greenberg

THEATRE COMMUNICATIONS GROUP
NEW YORK
2014

The Assembled Parties is copyright © 2014 by Richard Greenberg

The Assembled Parties is published by Theatre Communications Group, Inc., 520 Eighth Avenue, 24th Floor, New York, NY 10018-4156

All rights reserved. Except for brief passages quoted in newspaper, magazine, radio or television reviews, no part of this book may be reproduced in any form or by any means, electronic or mechanical, including photocopying or recording, or by an information storage and retrieval system, without permission in writing from the publisher.

Professionals and amateurs are hereby warned that this material, being fully protected under the Copyright Laws of the United States of America and all other countries of the Berne and Universal Copyright Conventions, is subject to a royalty. All rights, including but not limited to, professional, amateur, recording, motion picture, recitation, lecturing, public reading, radio and television broadcasting, and the rights of translation into foreign languages are expressly reserved. Particular emphasis is placed on the question of readings and all uses of this book by educational institutions, permission for which must be secured from the author's representative: George Lane, Creative Artists Agency, 405 Lexington Avenue, 19th Floor, New York, NY 10174, (212) 277-9000.

The publication of *The Assembled Parties*, by Richard Greenberg, through TCG's Book Program, is made possible in part by the New York State Council on the Arts with the support of Governor Andrew Cuomo and the New York State Legislature.

TCG books are exclusively distributed to the book trade by Consortium Book Sales and Distribution.

LIBRARY OF CONGRESS CATALOGING-IN-PUBLICATION DATA
Greenberg, Richard, 1958– author.
The assembled parties / Richard Greenberg.—First edition.
pages cm
ISBN 978-1-55936-476-8 (paperback)
ISBN 978-1-55936-788-2 (ebook)
I. Title.
PS3557.R3789A86   2014
812'.54—dc23   2014019207

Book design and composition by Lisa Govan
Cover design by Mark Melnick

First Edition, November 2014

The Assembled Parties *was written for Jessica Hecht, Judith Light, and Lynne Meadow*

How Theater Is Like
a Hostage Situation

By Richard Greenberg

Years ago, I saw a play that was beautifully written, superbly acted and hell to sit through.

It started with a character announcing that nothing was going to happen. Then she rattled off a list of examples of what wouldn't be happening; they were the sorts of interesting-sounding things that typically happen in plays in which things happen.

It was easy enough for me to figure out why I was having such a terrible time: Nothing was happening. But to keep from hyperventilating, I started to wonder about things other than the play, as it was refusing to unfold. One of these was whether, given the fine acting and beautiful writing—by this I mean beautiful sentences; it was a parade of lovely, inert sentences—were there conditions under which I could watch this play without wanting to kill myself?

The answer was yes and came quite easily: I would be fine if I could walk around.

Maria Irene Fornes's *Fefu and Her Friends* came to mind, though not perhaps aptly, as things happen in *Fefu and Her Friends*. Still, it seemed to me that if these scenes to which I was being subjected were enacted in, say, a house that I could wander through, pausing and listening at will, I might have been having a tolerable, even a delightful experience.

This made me ponder (because, trust me, there was still a lot of time to kill) the conditions under which we traditionally watch plays: crammed into uncomfortable seats, plunged into darkness, enjoined to remain silent, and suffering censure if we protest in any way.

Clearly, what going to the theater most closely resembled was a hostage situation, and this explained the extremity of my reaction. The enforced stillness of my role as an audience member created in me an anxiety for action. It seemed plausible to posit this as a law: Because the audience cannot move, the play must.

I believe this is why when we hate a play, we hate it so much more desperately than we do a movie or a novel or a painting. When we watch a play under the standard circumstances, we've lost volition and time is passing. A stalled play feels like an existential threat. Arguably, the story under the story of every play is just that: Time is passing. The master playwrights of the twentieth century—Chekhov, Strindberg, Beckett, add your favorite—were superb at exploiting the theater's potential to excruciate time.

In a way, the bad evening at the play that traveled at the speed of stop helped me understand why I write plays: I've always been obsessed with time—not in a profound way, but with what it *feels* like. There's a game I play with myself—or maybe it's a disorder. This is how it goes:

I think: "When as much time passes as has passed since (some year that I remember well), I will be (_____) years old." It's been especially interesting since the answer started to come up "dead."

The Assembled Parties, is set on two Christmases in 1980 and 2000. It's anti-Aristotelian, reveling in disunities of time and action—though it's pretty good about place. The idea of a rupture between acts occurs in a number of my plays. It's a method I can trace back to the event that had a formative influence on my sensibility: a PBS pledge drive. I'll explain.

When I was a little kid, there was a black-and-white, video-taped miniseries from England based on John Galsworthy's *The Forsyte Saga*. Shown here, it was a sensation, the event that turned PBS into Britain's last colonial outpost in the U.S.

I liked it at the time. It was filled with chuffy English acting and the young Susan Hampshire, and I was an annoying premature Anglophile (that faded). What was not to like?

A decade or so later, in an effort to drum up money, the series was rerun as a marathon. I think it went a solid day. I was visiting home from one university or another and I found myself checking in at irregular intervals. A baby would be born. I'd rake some leaves. When I returned, twenty years had gone by and that baby had just been killed in The Great War. I watched the whole series in that stertorous way.

It was devastating.

Accelerated and gapped, it accorded precisely with my newly kindled (I was in my early twenties) sense of reality: Time was implacable, events whizzed by, and *I didn't have all the information.*

In the first act of *The Assembled Parties*, Santo Loquasto's set—a vast apartment on the Upper West Side—spins from room-to-room. In each room, something happens that is or isn't or sort-of-is related to what happens in the other rooms. Families of good will (they exist) are failed attempts at a common pursuit. I've written the play so that the audience possesses the necessary facts, the characters don't completely. Twenty years pass in the blink of an intermission and all the wisdom, care and anxiety of the first act seem to have been misapplied; what's been prepared for is not what's happened. Everyone tries to adjust.

And time remains implacable.

This essay was previously published by Broadway.com on March 26, 2013.

The
Assembled
Parties

Production History

The world premiere of *The Assembled Parties* was presented on Broadway at the Samuel J. Friedman Theatre by Manhattan Theatre Club (Lynne Meadow, Artistic Director; Barry Grove, Executive Director) on April 17, 2013. It was directed by Lynne Meadow; the set design was by Santo Loquasto, the costume design was by Jane Greenwood, the lighting design was by Peter Kaczorowski, the sound design and original music were by Obadiah Eaves; the production stage manager was Barclay Stiff. The cast was:

JULIE	Jessica Hecht
FAYE	Judith Light
JEFF	Jeremy Shamos
MORT	Mark Blum
SHELLEY	Lauren Blumenfeld
TIMMY	Alex Dreier
SCOTTY/TIM	Jake Silbermann
BEN	Jonathan Walker
VOICE OF HECTOR	Gabriel Sloyer

CHARACTERS

JULIE
FAYE
JEFF
MORT
SHELLEY
TIMMY/TIM
SCOTTY
BEN
VOICE OF HECTOR

Scotty and Tim are played by the same actor.

PLACE

A fourteen-room apartment on Central Park West.

TIME

Act One: Christmas Day, 1980.
Act Two: Christmas Day, 2000.

Notes

The first act moves swiftly among suggestions of rooms.

The second act resolves into a detailed box set, inert, depicting the living room and, recessed, the dining room.

A slash (/) in dialogue indicates when the next actor starts speaking.

Act One

———

Christmas Day, 1980

The kitchen. Food. Julie and Jeff.

JULIE: Yes! Yes! Yes! Yes!
    Oh lovely!
    That would be so lovely!
JEFF: Good.
JULIE: Are you sophisticated at this sort of thing?
JEFF: I have no skills
JULIE: None needed—are you safe with a chef's knife?
JEFF: I love to cut things
JULIE: These vegetables
JEFF *(Continuous)*: I don't mean in a Norman Bates sort of
    way—I like being a sous chef—
JULIE: Cut them crosswise—medium and then toss them in
    that bowl of water so they don't get mange, okay?
JEFF: What is this going to be
JULIE: Oh that's part crudité—part mirepoix—and this is going
    to be rumaki— Rumaki? Like from eons ago? The *six*ties

JEFF: That's liver?

JULIE: Yes, and for the main we're having a goose!

JEFF: I've never had a goose

JULIE: Oh! You coat the potatoes in semolina, then fry them in the drippings—it's medieval, there should be vassals and broadswords and a *may*pole

JEFF: Ha!

JULIE: How is your room; are you settled? Do you like it?

JEFF: After the dorm, it's pretty amazing

JULIE: Stay if you want, it's so remote you can hole up there for decades we won't even know.

JEFF: Tempting but . . .

JULIE: Obligations obligations

JEFF: Yes

JULIE: The Pressure to Become Something; Scotty, too

JEFF: Scotty espec / ially

JULIE: Graduation, I cried and cried; touching so touching, all of you—so witty, so oblique, so overeducated, so utterly ignorant of *ab*solutely *ev*erything.

(Beat.)

JEFF: I *guess*.

JULIE: It's so lovely Christmas.

Though you find that all the dying tends to accelerate around now.

And of course there's Bing Crosby.

JEFF: Bing Crosby?

JULIE: He's a tribulation, don't you find?

And you can't escape him!

To the Optimo Cigar Store for a five-cent stamp

and he's dreaming of a white Christmas.

It's like a tiny acoustic *rape* every time you leave the apartment.

But other than Bing Crosby and all that dying, it's a lovely, lovely season.

JEFF: Yes.

(He chops.)

Is someone dying?

JULIE: My husband's mother, most likely

JEFF: She's dying.

JULIE: We can't get a *time*table on it—she might linger even *years*—but, the smart money says kaput.

JEFF: I'm sorry.

Is she very old?

JULIE: Only eighty-seven.

JEFF: Oh!

JULIE: But she's an old eighty-seven.

JEFF: Is there such a thing as a young

JULIE: Come around when *I'm* eighty-seven; I'm going to be practically prepubes / cent.

JEFF: I bet.

But should I *be* here?

JULIE: Certainly. Why not?

JEFF: Things you need to do and . . . I'll be in the way?

(Beat.)

JULIE: You haven't had a lot of people die, have you?

JEFF: None.

JULIE: That changes.

You get to a point there's always somebody.

You have to be hardheaded about it, you have to go about your business. A cheerful nature is an utterly ruthless thing.

JEFF: You're not ruthless.

JULIE: I'm the most ruthless woman you'll ever meet.

I'm diabolical. *(She smiles)*

JEFF: I'm so glad I'm here!

JULIE: Oh, you're lovely, aren't you? Just lovely.

JEFF *(Bursting)*: *Thank* you.

JULIE: Scotty's friends are all so nice.

JEFF *(Disappointed)*: Oh.

(Ben enters.)

BEN: Why aren't you drinking?

JEFF: It's still kind of / early

JULIE: How is Timmy? Did you

BEN: Subsiding

JULIE: Oh my! I don't think I like the sound of

BEN: The fever, sweetie, the fever; sleeping like a

JULIE: Is he still flushed

BEN: He's *four*; they're always flushed

JULIE: You're useless—useless man!

BEN: Scotty's still in the / shower?

JULIE: Still in the / shower

BEN: Christ! The Rappaports haven't called / have they?

JULIE: Slightly larger cuts, sweetheart—I'm sure they're on the road by now

BEN: You know Faye—if traffic's bad, they'll pull off and phone from, I don't know, the Fiorello LaGuardia Memorial Rest Stop—how would you like to have a rest stop named after you? I mean, do we think that's actually an honor—

JEFF: I doubt I'll ever be distinguished enough to have a rest stop named after me.

BEN: That's always seemed a backhanded compliment

JEFF: I'm trying for a urinal, you know, if I step things up—

BEN: HA! That's funny.

JEFF: . . . Oh.

BEN: You're funny.

　　You should come visit us this summer.

　　In Nantucket.

JEFF: I would love to.

BEN: So now: Let's *talk* to you—are there nuts, by the

JULIE *(Slides bowl to him)*: Don't eat them / all

8

BEN: So then: the Law.

JEFF: Yes. Well . . . *yes.*

BEN: Do you love the Law in a . . . an Oliver Wendell

JEFF: No. Absolutely not.

BEN: I see. Then what do you

JEFF: It's a delaying tactic

BEN: Ah! So.

JEFF: Also it's a good basis.
　　　Like for anything.
　　　Everything's still a little
　　　um
　　　scintillating?
　　　And this is a way to have whatever skills I may
　　　need when I finally
　　　. . . whatever.

JULIE: When you find your heart's desire.

JEFF: . . . My heart's desire. Yes.

(They smile at each other.)

BEN: You like Boston?

JEFF: It's Cambridge, really,
　　　I *like* Cambridge.
　　　Cambridge is fun; you keep thinking
　　　something might *happen* in Cambridge.
　　　Also, you're walking from Torts to . . . lunch
　　　and it hits you:
　　　This is where Howells fought with James and—

JULIE: You're literary?
　　　Do you want to write?
　　　Ultimately? Lawyer-writer?
　　　Like Louis Auchincloss.

JEFF: No I'm just a reader

JULIE: All writers are readers; you sell yourself short.

JEFF: I don't

JULIE: You do

JEFF *(Beaming because she's interested in him)*: I have absolutely no abilities

BEN: I was expecting Scotty'd be there with you

JEFF: Oh.

Yes.

Well, deferred.

BEN: I was really *counting* on that.

JEFF: You're not . . . worried, about him are you?

JULIE: No.

BEN: To a degree.

JULIE: No of course not.

BEN: The question with Scotty has always been: Has he inherited his mother's aleatory qualities?

JEFF: Aleatory?

BEN: Haphazard, windblown, fortuitous

JULIE: Thank you for the endorsement, / darling

JEFF: I don't think so.

Scott's very *stea*dy?

Anyway I don't think you have to worry about, you know, his electability—the presidency is safe.

(Pause.)

BEN: Are you making fun?

JEFF: . . . No.

BEN: I think you are.

JEFF: Truly, I

BEN: Okay, you can forget about the summer—

JEFF: I

JULIE: He's joking, pay no attention; it's just that he's the most wretched man who ever drew breath

BEN: Every boy's parents want him to be president.

What? Don't yours?

JEFF: I . . . *doubt* it.

BEN: No? What do they want you to be?

JEFF: . . . Solvent?

BEN: So they're: Whatever makes him happy.

JEFF: Um? I think they'd be *fine* with me being happy?

　　But I'm not like—

　　I don't give off the sense that I'm destined to be

　　the first Jew on paper currency since Lincoln. Ha, ha.

BEN: What, you think in twenty-five years we won't be ready?

　　That's a hangover from my parents' generation.

　　Trust me in a quarter-century he won't be the first.

JEFF: It's inconceivable that he would be

　　. . . The second maybe.

BEN: . . . Not that I'm copping to your premise.

　　Scotty can be a beachcomber for all I—

JEFF: Sure: Gauguin.

BEN: Or a guy playing with coconuts.

　　He's his own man

　　. . .

　　It's a family joke: the "president."

　　A gag.

(Beat.)

JULIE: Is it?

(Beat.)

BEN: Why do I keep eating these?

JULIE: Because you lack control.

(He slides the bowl of nuts away.)

JEFF: I think I've cut every vegetable.

JULIE: And like an *art*isan!

JEFF: I should probably go call my parents

JULIE: Oh your lovely parents! I *wish* they'd been able to come.

　　They know they were invited, don't / they?

JEFF: Yeah, oh yeah, they just . . . you know

JULIE: I know. *Next* year.

JEFF: Maybe so. Well, I'll—

BEN *(Abrupt)*: Tell us about Scotty's girlfriend!

JEFF: Oh Ilana? She's amazing.

JULIE: You don't blunderbuss your / way into that topic

BEN: Scotty's gonna come out of the shower *one* of these days; seize the opportunity

JULIE: God.

JEFF: You've never met her?

BEN: She's always someplace else.

JULIE: She always seems to have other accommodations

BEN: This business of skipping her graduation

JEFF: Her summer program started / before grad—

JULIE: Her parents are very international, / I think?

JEFF: Yeah, she's amazing . . .

> She's coming tonight, right?

BEN: We *trust*

JULIE: Our fingers are crossed.

> You met her before Scotty did, didn't

JEFF: We were in the same Twentieth / Century History class.

BEN: She's very pretty in the one photograph we've been vouchsafed

JEFF: Yes: spectacular. Extraordinary, unprecedented. It's very hard to concentrate in lecture.

BEN: . . . Ah.

JULIE: How did you—

JEFF: Well. She made this statement? In class?

> That I thought was . . .
>
> Anyway, she made this rem*ark* that the Holocaust was the most sentimental event of the twentieth century.
>
> Which I thought was bullsh . . . *bull*

JULIE: Yes, that's not a new theory.

JEFF: Which, oh okay, I guess I was *wrong* about.

> But I didn't *real*ize that at the *time*, so
>
> I went up to her and *erroneously* told her that I thought what she said was . . .
>
> bull.

And I was really proud because she was scary and not just because of her unbelievable um beauty.

But she just looked at me.

And laughed. But not in a mean way, in this kind of "good for you, I like you. You've got bal . . . moxie" way?

And she kissed me.

It was the most amazing thing.

So I introduced her to Scotty.

And the rest is . . . and so forth.

She knows how to build a bomb!

JULIE: I don't understand.

JEFF: One time, for class, she built this bomb?

She showed it to me in my dorm room.

She said, "Guess what I've got?"

And then she took out this *bomb* that she had built. Like for extra credit?

I mean, it was just the three of us: me, a beautiful girl, and this *bomb*. It was . . . *utter.*

Later, she told me she didn't actually have the, um, full, the incendiary? The accelerant or—*the thing that would make it detonate.* But still it was, like, the greatest moment.

I just felt so *crisp.*

(Beat.)

JULIE: My.

JEFF: You shouldn't take that story to be indicative?

JULIE: What we're *wond*ering is

BEN: Is he gonna marry her? *That's* what we're

JULIE: Let's not skip steps: Is it, would you say, a great love?

Would you say it was an amour fou?

JEFF: Um.

Well.

I would definitely say it's an amour.

I don't know how fou it is.

BEN: He seems distracted.

Less motivated than I'd like.

He still hasn't knuckled under to going to law school next year or serious paying work.

He's just . . . / adrift.

JULIE: No the thing is you know, we haven't met the girl and while she certainly seems very interesting in your description, we're afraid he might sort of whimsically elope with her some evening for lack of a conflicting appointment.

JEFF: . . .

I don't know.

In a way, it's hard to imagine Ilana doing anything that . . . um . . . *legal?*

But you never know.

. . .

Why?

Do you want me to find out for you?

BEN: No, no, not at all.

JULIE *(Simultaneous with Ben above)*: Goodness, no! That's not what we're suggesting.

(That's exactly what they're suggesting. Pause. They stand around in it, caught. Doorbell rings.)

The Rappaports!

JEFF: I'm gonna call my parents.

(He exits.)

We go to the vestibule. Mort, Faye, Shelley, Julie, Ben.

MORT: What's news, what's news?

JULIE: Hey, there!

SHELLEY: Hi-i-i-i

FAYE: Are we interrupting?

JULIE: Not at all.

> Oh, you all look so pretty! Shelley, look at you! You've lost a person and I love your *Doctor Zhivago* hat.

SHELLEY: Thanks.

JULIE: You have a face that can carry it.

FAYE: You cooking? It smells am*bro*sial.

(Meanwhile hugs, coats collected.)

JULIE: I am: You know me, the / kitchen slut.

BEN: How was the traffic, Mort?

MORT: Not so bad. I took the Midtown / Tunnel.

FAYE: I love what you're wearing, Julie.

JULIE: This?

> Oh, thanks.

FAYE: Is it your mother's?

JULIE: Yes.

> Vintage.

FAYE: You can tell.

> Her designs.

> They have a signature.

> Yet they're so contemporary

JULIE: Do you think?

FAYE: Timeless.

> She was timeless.

> Take the babka.

JULIE: Oh! Babka! My favorite!

FAYE: Is Timmy still with the sniffles?

JULIE: He *is*. Poor tyke. But starting to feel better.

FAYE: We've brought him comic books

JULIE: Oh, *thank* you— Isn't that great?

FAYE: Maybe later we'll take a peek, he's so adorable

JULIE: He's pretty cute

BEN *(Simultaneous with above)*: There's something I want to give you, Mort.

MORT: Okay

FAYE: And Scotty?

JULIE: Showering, I think?

FAYE: Give? What are you giving?

BEN: Something for Mort.

FAYE: What?

BEN: It's a surprise

FAYE: Uh-huh . . . I need to talk to you, Benny.

BEN: Okay.

FAYE *(Simultaneous with above)*: Julie, is it okay if I talk to Benny?

JULIE: Yes I need to look in on my little boy. / Then cooking cooking cooking

BEN: Mort, Shelley, set yourselves up in the living room. There's—what—pigs-in-the-blanket?

JULIE: *Pigs*-in-the-blank—oh there are actually!

(And on the waft of her laughter, they disperse. Shelley has just stood there the entire time.)

A sitting room with a bar. Faye and Ben.

FAYE: I don't know at this point—I just don't know anymore.

BEN: What is there to say?

FAYE: It's like a "What's the worst that could happen?" joke

BEN: I agree

FAYE: He wasn't even a good actor. And he wasn't really handsome. He was B-movie handsome. I couldn't believe it when they made him Governor of California, and those people don't care *what* they do. But this: Leader of the Free / World

BEN: Things turn around.

FAYE: But in four years—the damage!

BEN: We'll organize

FAYE: Who? You and me?

BEN: Sure.

FAYE: Nonsense.

BEN: Of course it's nonsense; I *meant* it as / nonsense

FAYE: And who's *left* to organize?

> The Jews? The Jews are all turncoats. "Republican Jews"—
>
> What is that? It's like "skinny fat people."
>
> The kids? *These* kids? Scotty?

BEN: Scotty marched.

FAYE: Where did Scotty march?

BEN: At Princeton. Divestment from South Africa—

FAYE: Divestment at Princeton. Seven sophomores at lunch hour, round and round they go. Please. Sometimes I think the war ending was the worst thing that could have happened

BEN: Bite your tongue

FAYE: No one feels imperiled on a bodily level anymore. I'm just grateful I'm apolitical. And thank God Moishe and Bernice are dead, they'd be spitting nails if they saw what was happening. I'm *fear*ful.

BEN: Don't pull your Cassandra crap, Faye.

FAYE: Cassandra was *right*. Nudnik. That's the whole *point* of

BEN: Do you want a drink?

FAYE: A bissel vodka.

BEN *(Gets her drink)*: You seem agitated

FAYE: *This* is good by contemporary standards.

BEN: I hate to hear that.

> What does Dr. . . . . Erlich?

FAYE: Eren / reich

BEN: Erenreich! Say?

FAYE: I don't know. Who knows?

(She starts fiddling absently with tchotchkes on the table.)

> He finds my nostalgia for Miltown winsome.
>
> Life was so good during Miltown, Benny

BEN: Maybe there's some new

FAYE: That's the hope

BEN: Well then

FAYE: But let's not reduce me to this. I'm not a House of Chemicals, I'm a person coping with real-life issues that persist and gnaw and what is all this goyishe chazerai I'm playing with here?

BEN: Season's Greetings. Julie likes tchotchkes.

FAYE: Mom would have a knipsh.

Good for Julie—provocateuse.

Mom never liked her anyway.

BEN: She liked Julie.

FAYE: Only as a *person*. Not as an *entity*.

BEN: Rivka on the German Jews was a case for Menninger's.

FAYE: "The worst Jews in the world."

BEN: "Yes, Mom. And the fewest."

FAYE: That never somehow got to her. She didn't stumble over that.

BEN: She was a complicated woman.

FAYE: *Is*.

BEN: . . .

To a degree.

FAYE: Go. Go to her.

BEN *(Sighs)*: I am.

FAYE: She's *dy*ing

BEN: She's been dying as long as we've known her

FAYE: Now she's dying *worse*. When are you going?

BEN: Tomorrow.

FAYE: That's all I wanted to know.

BEN: Thank you.

FAYE: Because if you *don't*, God help you.

BEN: I said I'd go. Stop hoching me.

FAYE: And what do you have for Mort all of a sudden?

BEN: I've got this box of Havanas that

FAYE: Really? Why?

BEN: I can't give my brother-in-law a box of cigars?

FAYE: After thirty years? No.

BEN: You're a termagant.

FAYE: I don't like the sound of these Havanas.

BEN: So what are these real-life problems that are

FAYE: What?

BEN: What are these real-life problems that are at the "root of your malaise."

FAYE: Ugh, I don't want to talk about them

   . . .

   Shelley.

BEN: She looks terrific. She's lost a lot of weight.

FAYE: She troubles me.

BEN: Has it ever occurred to you you underestimate her?

FAYE: Every benefit of the doubt has been extended.

   I'm terrified something will happen to us—

   Terrified? You don't need an actuary: Eventually something *will* happen to us and who's going to take care of her? The Temple?

BEN: Does she—don't jump down my throat, Faye—does she date?

FAYE: . . . Others at her level.

BEN: So?

FAYE: I don't want her to be one of those couples—the Patronized: Isn't it nice? They *found* each other. People like that, they find each other, they compound the oddness.

BEN: This is all exaggeration, Faye.

FAYE: I don't know anything about her. What she does.

   The gynecologist won't tell / me.

BEN: Oh God, Faye.

FAYE: She's thirty years old.

   She *goes* places.

   Dances and Temple . . . sponsored . . . dances . . .

   That sort

   I mean . . .

   Do they even know what goes into what?

BEN: Have you talked to her about contraception?

FAYE: Imagine that discussion, Ben.

>   She's an oppressor. She oppresses me.

>   When will it lift?

BEN: It will lift

FAYE: But *when?*

BEN: That I can't tell you.

(Beat.)

FAYE: She knows how long you haven't been.

BEN: Shelley?

FAYE: Don't kid. Mom.

BEN: Mad as a hatter, fogbound in senility, and she

FAYE: The sense of neglect is the last to go

BEN: You're a pisser, / Faye—

FAYE: You haven't met the woman?

>   You go to see her, she's in a coma, she's *dead*, she'll wake
>   up expressly to make you feel terrible

BEN *(Sighs)*: Our mother.

FAYE: A genius of affrontedness.

BEN: . . . When did you last visit?

FAYE: Two days ago.

BEN: Was she

FAYE: Suddenly she wakes up geshrying about Ruchel.

BEN: Oh God.

FAYE: And somebody named Duvid and a *dance* of all things

BEN: What dance?

FAYE: What do I know? The *prom.*

>   Who knew in Galicia they were going to dances and
>   stealing each other's boyfriends? I thought they were too
>   busy toiling.

>   They put her in restraints.

BEN: What?

FAYE: A mini-straitjack / et

BEN: I'll sue

FAYE: You're not suing, she was violent

BEN: She weighs four ounc / es

FAYE: She's grabbing the attendants, shaking them, she's a broken sparrow of a woman with the grip of Rocky Marciano.

BEN: Jesus. "Do Not Go Gentle into That Good / Night"

FAYE: And has there ever been a more useless piece of advice? *Who* goes gentle into that good night? Certainly none of *our* relatives.

Those White Horse Tavern drunks, trust me: I knew them; they were shmucks; don't listen to anything they say.

BEN *(Referring to the vodka)*: Do you want another?

FAYE: I'm saving room for a sedative. *(Pause)* What was the point, Benny?

BEN: I don't know, Faye.

FAYE: Why did our mother choose me for an enemy?

Who benefited?

BEN: No one.

FAYE: And say she dies.

Does that mean it's over or that
it's never over?

BEN: . . . There'll be a pill eventually.

(Jeff wanders in.)

JEFF: Oh! Sorry!

I didn't mean to inter / rupt

BEN: You're not—

JEFF: I was looking for Scotty's room—I can't get the hang of this place, it's very big

FAYE *(Snapping out of her mood, social performance)*: It's *very* big

BEN: Have you met?

FAYE *(Continuous)*: Remember, Ben, Gussie, describing when she was brand-new in America?

BEN: Sure

FAYE: "It's a bewilderness," she said

BEN: A bewilderness

FAYE: I felt it too, twenty years ago: *here.*

Come often enough, you'll figure it out.

There are only six or seven dozen rooms

BEN: Fourteen, four of them / small

FAYE: I'm Faye the sister.

JEFF: I'm Jeff.

FAYE: Scotty's friend from school.

JEFF: Yes.

FAYE: Nice to meet / you

JEFF: Nice to meet *you.*

I think your husband was wandering in some hallway
looking for Mr. Bascov.

BEN: Ben.

JEFF: For yes *(Mutters)* Ben.

BEN: I'll find him

(Shelley wanders in.)

SHELLEY: Hi.

FAYE: Why are you here, Shelley?

SHELLEY: I was in the bathroom. I *still get lost* in this apart /
ment

BEN: You haven't met Jeff, have you?

SHELLEY: Who?

BEN: This is our houseguest, Jeff Bornstein.

He also gets lost.

JEFF: I do.

FAYE: You have that in common.

BEN: I'm going to talk to your dad now

FAYE: I need to talk to Julie.

JEFF: Nice to meet you.

SHELLEY: Nice to meet you

FAYE: She's back in the kitchen, right?

JEFF: I think so. I can look if you—

FAYE: No no, sit, sit.

JEFF: I also need to call my

22

FAYE *(Simultaneous with Jeff above)*: You two young people talk.

(Faye and Ben go.)

JEFF: I—oh. *(Sees he's alone with Shelley)*

(Shelley sits.)

Oh. *(Now he must too. At length)*
　　So . . . Do you . . . go to school?
SHELLEY *(Unhinged laughter)*: College? No! *(It abates)*
JEFF: . . . Oh.
SHELLEY: I work at Alexander's.
JEFF: Oh! That's nice.
SHELLEY: Yeah
JEFF: . . .
　　The one in King's Plaza?
SHELLEY: Roosevelt Field.
JEFF: Oh!
　　Of course.
　　Roosevelt Field.
SHELLEY: Yeah.
JEFF: I've been to
　　—I mean, I know it well, of course.
　　I loved it when I was a child.
SHELLEY: Yeah. Roosevelt Field Mall.

(Beat.)

JEFF: So is that your
　　primary . . . area of interest?
　　Retail?
SHELLEY: I don't mind.
　　Long as every Thursday my paycheck's in my pocket
　　I'm happy.

JEFF: . . . Exactly.

There's so much romance about "work," isn't there, but essentially it's utilitarian.

(Beat. She looks at him.)

I've always thought malls were the romance of the suburbs, do you know? The randomness of a city, but in a *container*.

(She looks at him.)

Do you like it?

SHELLEY: I don't mind. My parents, though! They don't like it when they have to park.

JEFF: Yes! The parking is notor / ious.

SHELLEY: Oh my mother especially: She don't like it at all.

She says, Why can't you take the bus?

I say, When the bus runs my hours I'll take the bus.

And my father! He just swears. He's got a terrible mouth on him

JEFF: I have a friend who proposed that as a road test, you take the kid to Roosevelt Field on a Saturday and if he lives, he passes.

SHELLEY: That'd be dangerous though.

(Beat.)

JEFF: She was joking.

SHELLEY: It's *crazy* there.

(Beat.)

JEFF: Yes . . .

SHELLEY: You're Scotty's friend?

JEFF: Yes!

SHELLEY: You must be smart, then

JEFF: . . . It's a matter of . . . application more than

SHELLEY: 'Cause Scotty's smart.

He's always been smart from the time he was born, Scotty.

My father says to me: How can you have a cousin's so smart when you're such a dummy?

JEFF: . . . He . . . doesn't . . . say that

SHELLEY: I say, I don't know 'cause I'm too dumb.

He don't have *noth*ing to say to that.

JEFF: . . . Touché . . .

SHELLEY: Yeah. Everybody always said Scotty's different. My father says, That Scotty's so pretty, too bad he's the boy and you're the girl.

(Jeff has nothing to say to that.)

I was never school-smart.

JEFF: Who's to say?

SHELLEY *(Continuous)*: I have common *sense*

JEFF: Which is rare. *(Is anyone ever going to enter this room?)*

So

. . .

What do you want to *be*?

SHELLEY: Oh, I don't want to be nothin'.

As long as I get a paycheck every Thursday.

My father, he says, You got a good job. You don't ask them for a raise. They pay you what they think you're worth. Why rock the boat?

(Jeff is visibly distressed.)

JEFF: That *can't* be the time.

Oh shoot! I was supposed to—

Scotty and I—

Oh man—

Listen, I'll see you at dinner, yes?

We'll continue our—
I can't believe that's what *time* . . .
wish me luck finding his room!

(Jeff hastens out. Shelley just sits there. Nothing happens in her face or body. She sits some more.)

Scotty's bedroom. Scotty, post-shower, is in a hotel robe, lying down on his bed. Jeff enters.

JEFF: What the fuck are you doing—hiding?
SCOTTY: Hey! Hi. No
JEFF: Because your entire family has arrived in a pack
SCOTTY: They're already here?
JEFF: Yeah.
SCOTTY: Shit, I'm gonna have to
JEFF: Right, *right.*
        But: your cousin?
SCOTTY: Poor Shelley.
        Why? Did you have an *episode* with her?
JEFF: I wandered into this room and then she . . . like . . . *wandered* into the same room—this place is, like, you need a Sherpa—and we were somehow *thrust* upon each other
SCOTTY: Oh fuck
JEFF: And a really riveting, Noël Coward–like conversation ensued
SCOTTY: Did Aunt Faye like ar*range* for you / to
JEFF: Maybe?
SCOTTY: Babe, I think you're engaged.
JEFF: Oh, they're posting the banns, no question
SCOTTY: I'll be your Best Man
JEFF: You will stand beside me under the ch-ch-chuppa

SCOTTY: At Temple Beth Yikes
JEFF: I'm buying my *tallit* and my *payus* / as we speak
SCOTTY: Mazel
JEFF: I'm plotzing.

(They laugh a little.)

SCOTTY *(Contrition)*: She's a nice girl, though. I don't like to . . .
JEFF: . . . No . . . no . . .
SCOTTY: God, they're here already
JEFF: I can attest
SCOTTY *(Sighs)*: I guess I'm gonna have to . . . present myself
JEFF: Are you getting Timmy's flu? You look
SCOTTY: I'm okay. God, I'm a shitty host—I just abandoned you
JEFF: You have
SCOTTY: Have you been holed up in / your
JEFF: No—I've been talking to your folks, actually, it's
SCOTTY: You have
JEFF: Oh! By the way? I love your mom.
       I hope you don't mind but I'm marrying your mom.
SCOTTY: What's mine is yours.
JEFF: I figured that. But you know, I like to be appropriate.
SCOTTY: And what about my dad?
JEFF: He'll have to bow out gracefully.
SCOTTY: How does he seem to you?
JEFF: Um
SCOTTY: I mean, does he seem different in any way
JEFF: I don't have, like, that much of a *base*line
SCOTTY: Right
JEFF: He's the way he's supposed to be.
       Like when I researched your family:
          "He possesses a management style at once humane and
       terrifying."
SCOTTY: Something's going on with him.
JEFF: Like what?
SCOTTY: Like he says, "Hi, Scott."

And he's really stern about it.

And then he gets, like, yielding?

And then it's like he's going to cry or something.

JEFF: And this is: "Hi, Scott"?

SCOTTY: Has he asked you anything about me?

JEFF: Asked me about you?

No. What do you mean?

SCOTTY: I'm not trying to turn you into a *spy* or anything like that but he's not a subtle man, he would interrogate you; he *does* that.

JEFF: Well . . . he hasn't.

SCOTTY: Wow. Good.

JEFF: Yeah. *(They nod)* So are you gonna marry Ilana?

SCOTTY: *Par*don?

JEFF: Like on the hoof? Like elope to Vegas or Biafra or someplace romantic / like that?

SCOTTY: Where did *that* idea come from?

JEFF: I dunno. The question just seemed to be in the air

SCOTTY: Really: You and Shelley will be happening before / Ilana and

JEFF: She's coming, though, right? Tonight? Ilana?

SCOTTY: Who the fuck knows?

Probably not.

The last time I en*treat*ed her, she said / not

JEFF: *Why?*

SCOTTY: I dunno. She's got a *cold* or the *patriarchy*; something

JEFF: Did you fuck up on the trip or something?

SCOTTY: I don't *think* so. I don't know. *May*be. Jeez.

JEFF: Fuck

. . .

How was your trip anyway?

I should have asked but I wasn't really that interested.

How was . . . Rwanda or whatever?

SCOTTY: It was,

you know,

crappy but ennobling

or some shit like that

. . .

There were these people there—like *peace* workers?—
And I looked at them and *lis*tened and I thought:
I Am Not These People
and then I'd look at Ilana and think:
And Nor Are You

JEFF: And "neither"

SCOTTY: Huh?

JEFF: Not "and nor"—"and neither."

But—no—go on—

SCOTTY: Yeah—right—no: *Thank* you—but

JEFF: Right

SCOTTY: It really made me look at my whole relationship with
Ilana, you know? Because hasn't the whole premise been
that she's a pain in the ass but by committing myself to
her I'll *transcend* my inbred uselessness?

JEFF: Uh-huh, right.

SCOTTY: But what if she's not authentic in *her* commitments?

What if she's just this . . . fucking lunatic?

Does it all really just come down to: Sex With A Crazy
Girl?

Which would be unbelievably dishonorable; do you
know?

JEFF: Okay.

Wow.

SCOTTY: Yeah.

JEFF: *Or* is it that *subconsciously* you're thinking, Holy shit, am
I dating Angela Davis and thirty years from now, how will
that play with the electorate?

SCOTTY: No, it isn't. *(He looks over his shoulder, then closes door)*

Jeff, I had this huge revelation.

JEFF: Oh God—on your trip?

SCOTTY: Even before—when I was writing my thesis.

JEFF *(With real concern)*: What is it?

SCOTTY: I'm not essentially political.

JEFF: . . . Wow.

SCOTTY: Which is, like, the opposite of all known facts concerning me and my, like, Destiny and shit?

JEFF: Right. Yeah.

SCOTTY: So I had to ask myself: What do I want to be, really?

JEFF: And: Have You An Answer?

SCOTTY: I'm thinking . . . maybe . . . a teacher?

(Jeff just looks at him for a long time.)

JEFF: A *teacher?*

SCOTTY: Yeah. I like kids . . . and reading . . . and I like explaining things . . . and . . . I . . .

(Beat.)

JEFF: This is BS, Scotty.

SCOTTY: I don't think so.

JEFF: You're just *tired* or something.

Come to Harvard next year with me then be President of the United States like a good boy.

SCOTTY: God I'm an asshole! I'm like: Me me me, I haven't even *asked:*

How *is* it?

JEFF: Oh—it's fantastic.

SCOTTY: Really?

JEFF: It's amazing.

SCOTTY: No kidding?

JEFF: You saw *The Paper Chase*: It's a Kafkaesque nightmare!

SCOTTY: Oh.

Do you see much of Caroline?

JEFF: . . . Not that much.

SCOTTY: Why not?

JEFF: You know, she's in the English department . . .

SCOTTY: Right.

Which is located on Harvard's *Detroit* campus?

JEFF: No, it's just . . . whatever . . .

And she's seeing a lot of this guy in the business school named Craig.

SCOTTY: Shit. I'm

JEFF: No, it's

SCOTTY: She's with this *lout* instead of

JEFF: Yeah.

Well, actually, he's a pretty good guy.

You know: As good as a guy in the business school named Craig *can* be

SCOTTY: Shit.

But you looked really happy with her.

JEFF: . . . Yeah

. . . So next year in Cambridge.

SCOTTY: Except I really don't think I want to be a lawyer.

JEFF: I *know* I don't want to be a lawyer.

But it's good for so many other things

SCOTTY: Such as?

JEFF: Not having to do anything else for three years

. . .

It's kinda lonely there?

Like there aren't any people really?

SCOTTY: You'll adjust.

It's only been one semester.

(Deflated beat.)

JEFF: So okay—even if she's psychotic and not coming to dinner, Ilana's still coming to the club with us, right?

SCOTTY: I think I'm a little wiped for the club, bud—

JEFF: But—

SCOTTY: You can go

JEFF: Without you?

SCOTTY: Yeah.

JEFF: That's preposterous.

SCOTTY: Why?

JEFF: They won't even let me through the *door*, Scotty

SCOTTY: You're absurd

JEFF: And what would I do even if they did?

     I mean: What would I do?

SCOTTY: . . . Take Ilana.

     She likes you better than she does me these / days, any

JEFF: Yeah, right

SCOTTY: Really, you have my blessing.

JEFF: . . .

     That'll never happen.

(Pause.)

(Sort of sad and irresolute) No, it's okay.

(Beat.)

     I've gotta call my parents

SCOTTY: Yeah, I wanna look in on Timmy, and it'll be dinner before you know it.

JEFF *(A joke)*: I presume we'll be dressing for dinner.

SCOTTY *(Not a joke)*: Yes.

JEFF: . . .

     What?

SCOTTY *(Shrugs)*: For Christmas, you know . . .

JEFF: You're—no—really?

SCOTTY: Well: Christmas. You brought a suit, right?

(They look at each other.)

JEFF *(As if it's a put-on, maybe)*: Right.

     Whatever.

A hallway. Jeff enters. He looks one way, the other.
Suddenly, from off:

BEN'S VOICE: *A fucking string of phony rubies!*

(Jeff is stilled by this.)

JEFF: What?

To kitchen. Faye and Julie sit at the table. Julie's hands clasp
Faye's. Faye has been crying but now has mastered it.

FAYE: I'm so sorry . . .

JULIE: No—*no*—

FAYE: I've always tried not to be the woman at the party having the nervous breakdown in the kitchen. It's been a
point of pride.

JULIE: No, Faye, you're going through a hard time.

FAYE: But you have so much to do: your goose.

JULIE: The goose is resting.

FAYE *(Nods)*: . . . I'm sure that means something.

JULIE: I'm all yours. *(Beat)* Your mother—do they know—
how long—

FAYE: A couple of weeks.

A couple of days.

Tonight.

JULIE: I'm so sorry.

FAYE: Ach, what's the difference?

I was her *chosen one*. Even more than Benny.

It was always like that.

Until Mort. Morty!

What can I say? I'm a person in a farce, that's all there
is to it.

JULIE: You aren't

FAYE: Morty was sitting at that bar, monosyllabic with the T-shirt, I was drunk, I assumed he was an Abstract Expressionist. Farce! Cold light of morning he turns out to be a boy from the neighborhood. Two blocks away: I never saw him.

Meanwhile, Shelley was started.

In the throes of a terrible misunderstanding.

I was so afraid when I told Rivka. I was trembling. Do you know what she did?

She offered me my choice of two underhanded doctors.

How she knew them I have no idea.

But I was afraid I'd die.

JULIE: Of course / you were

FAYE: I was afraid I'd die, Julie.

I was a *girl* from the neighborhood. Despite Hunter College.

Which ended, all at once.

I wasn't her chosen one anymore.

And the next thirty years she looked for ways to hurt me.

As if that's needed.

Mort. Shelley.

JULIE: But you love them. You love Mort.

FAYE: No.

That was never part of it on either side.

It's not a Tevye-Golde thing.

Thirty years pass.

"Do You Love Me?"

Not really.

What we have is a mutual appreciation of our situation.

We function.

We love *something*.

Order. The responsibilities entailed.

What? I should be like those dames in Great Neck, all of a sudden they've developed needs? Just so their husbands won't be able to fulfill them?

What would that get me?

So I divorce Morty:

Next day, Armand Assante sends me a bouquet of roses? It ain't happenin'.

I appreciate Morty's qualities.

He's a solid man.

But let's not insist on love.

The grand gesture? The little gesture? Not in him.

And when it comes to Shelley, I'm nothing short of a madwoman.

JULIE: You're *not* a madwoman. You're a lovely, bright, rational person who at the moment is going through a hard time.

FAYE: A *mad*woman.

Do you know what I did just now?

JULIE: What?

FAYE: I left her with that boy—that Scotty friend.

JULIE: *Jeff?*

FAYE: As if for a hemidemisemiquaver of time *that* could seem like a sensible thought? Madness!

What can we expect from me next? "Prime Minister Trudeau, have you met my daughter Shelley?"

JULIE: It probably won't go / that far.

FAYE: And the thing is, I'm not by nature a malcontent.

JULIE: I know you / aren't

FAYE: I've sought out the alleviations that were offered.

That ashram. Ridiculous. But I *went.*

JULIE: I remember.

FAYE: Two *years* in a consciousness-raising group.

Jesus—did you ever join a—

JULIE: No. I knew some of the actual people so I didn't need to

FAYE: Ignominious! Ig. No. *Min*ious!

I was hauling off to Hewlett, to Woodmere—

JULIE: Woodmere!

FAYE: These yentas and their rec rooms. And they'd send an "expert." "He never takes out the garbage," Sadie says. "Sadie here has an interesting point," says the expert. Oh yes. Would that Mary Wollstonecraft had had the benefit of Sadie; everything'd be different.

There was a newsletter: a solid field of exclamation points. Plus a poet-in-residence. I have her masterpiece by heart:

> They call us glib
> And Adam's Rib
> But here's the squib
> And it's no fib
> We're changin' the world
> With Women's Lib!

What was I supposed to do with that?

One night at McSorley's, I was ignored by e. e. cummings himself and they're giving me "here's the squib and it's no fib."

It was just a reminder of loss.

JULIE: No, Faye.

FAYE: What can I do?

I'm a character in a farce.

I'm *cursed. (A shuddering sigh)*

Your mother was cold, wasn't she?

JULIE: I don't know that I'd say she was cold, exactly.

Busy?

FAYE: But she wasn't out to wreck your life?

JULIE: Oh no—goodness, not at all.

FAYE: That's nice. It gives you a leg up.

JULIE: Yes. I've certainly had good luck.

FAYE: . . . You're a happy woman, aren't you?

JULIE *(Truly contrite)*: I'm so sorry.

FAYE: I don't begrudge you.

I don't under*stand* it—Benny, that *pischer.*

JULIE: He's your brother—it would be unseemly if you did under / stand.

FAYE: But everything you gave up.

JULIE: I didn't give up anything.

FAYE: The movies! You were a movie / star

JULIE: I was a teenager

FAYE: You were delightful.

JULIE: My main talent was not looking like Sandra Dee.

Or whoever was being Sandra Dee that year.

It was only four movies, isn't that *something*?

Just a phase, really.

I love that it happened to me but it was nothing to give up. And I've loved everything that's happened to me since just as much.

FAYE: You make it sound as if you never did anything on purpose.

JULIE: It's *been* like that.

I've always just been borne along to pleasant places.

FAYE *(Affectionately)*: You're a disgrace.

JULIE: I know—I'm a throwback, it's dreadful.

Terrible times—hell*a*cious times and

I've slipped between the cracks.

I'll surely burn for eternity.

But for now . . .

FAYE *(Wandered back to her own distress)*: But this is what I think, though. Tell me if you agree:

If you've *lost* someone—if someone is lost to you—hurting them is a way of *having* them.

Isn't it? A blow like a signature.

A *claim.*

Yes?

JULIE: . . . Yes. I'm sure / that's so

FAYE: So, in that case, to *wound* is to *love.*

Isn't it? Don't you think?

JULIE: I'm certain it is.

FAYE: Really? You agree?

JULIE: Yes. I do.

FAYE *(Bursting into tears)*: But it's the stupidest thing I've ever said!

JULIE: What can I *do?* How can I *help?*

FAYE *(Rummages through her bag)*: No, I'm fine, I can handle this. *(Rummages harder. Panic, then the dread realization. No longer crying, beyond that)* Oh God. Oh God.

JULIE: What?

FAYE: Julie—

JULIE: Yes?

FAYE: There's something you *can* do.

JULIE: Anything—

FAYE *(Urgent)*: Give me a *pill.*

JULIE: Oh—I'm sorry—*damn* it, I'm not depressed!

I've got nothing. Don't you have a pre*scrip*tion somewhere?

FAYE: How nutty I am these days—

I left the bottle in Roslyn.

You have to have *some*thing.

JULIE: . . . There might be a few Valium

FAYE: I'll take them

JULIE: But they're from when I was pregnant.

FAYE: With which?

JULIE: Timmy.

FAYE: Fine

JULIE: He's four, Faye.

FAYE: I'm no connoisseur, I won't notice if they're a little stale—

JULIE: What if they've gone poisonous?

I would hate for Christmas to turn into some bathetic Jackie Susann situation with you sprawled on the kitchen floor.

FAYE: *Do you want me to hate you the way everybody thinks I should?*

JULIE: I don't . . .

FAYE: Then gimme.

JULIE: Does everybody think you should hate me?

FAYE: Yes.

JULIE: Why?

FAYE: Don't be disingenuous, just pass me the Valium. *Please.*

(Julie reluctantly does. Faye starts unscrewing the lid.)

JULIE: Wait until I get you water at least—
FAYE: Water isn't necessary, water is a *garnish. (She swallows them. She's instantly calmer)*
JULIE: That's uncanny.
FAYE: This isn't calm; it's the anticipation of calm.

(Julie smiles uncertainly.)

The goose, on the other hand, looks perfectly at ease.
JULIE *(Calls out)*: Everybody get ready for dinner!
FAYE *(Calls)*: And that's you, too, Mort!

Library. Ben and Mort with drinks. They've been talking.

BEN: Yes. Well . . . Yes.
MORT: Sure. *Everything* was under the counter, then.
　　　When Faye worked at Goody's store, do you think he was paying taxes?
BEN: I dunno.
MORT: Every third day, the register was "broken."
　　　She wrote receipts by hand.
　　　She was making numbers up.
　　　That whole family. That's what they were like.
BEN: I suppose.

(They nod at each other. Pause. More a standoff, really.)

Are we going to continue this way?
MORT: What way is that?
BEN: Chitchatting in this *mode.*
MORT: I got nothin' else goin' on.

BEN: You've always been a brutal man, Mort.

(Beat.)

MORT: Okay.
BEN: Your whole family was
MORT: I know you think that.
BEN: Your father was a thug. And your mother—I don't even want to *name* what your mother was.

(Beat.)

MORT: My mother was a beautician.
BEN: In the *front* room.
MORT: People had loose lips.
BEN: I popped my cherry in the back room of that "beauty parlor" so you can drop the veneer with me.

(Beat.)

MORT: It was the Depression.
BEN: People were seamstresses.
 People were locksmiths.
 People had jobs sticking labels on dented cans.

(Beat.)

MORT: That was them.

(Beat.)

BEN: *A fucking string of phony rubies!*
MORT: You should lower your voice.
BEN: I can't believe you'd—I'm in*cred*ulous to think
 it's come to this—it's beyond the power of my imagina-
tion—

MORT: You don't have to imagine nothing. It's true.

BEN: If my sister knew what you were doing

MORT: But she won't.

BEN: Do you understand what *hokum* this is?

MORT: Nah, I don't see that, / Benny.

BEN: A ruby necklace—it's Agatha Chris—it's
Arsène Lupin! We're a potboiler here!
Snapshots? A private detective?

MORT: There's no pri / vate detective

BEN: This *spy*

MORT: A friend, a goddamn *Team*ster—

BEN: Teamsters! Morty . . . This is crazy.
You see me on the street. With some woman. In an
incautious moment.
Suddenly the world is upended?
I mean: Come on. I love Julie.
I love my wife.
I love my *family*.

MORT: Oh I know that, Benny. If you didn't, I wouldn't have
anything to work with here.

BEN: You're making something ruinous out of this nothing?

MORT: *N*othing? You think that's *nothing*?

BEN: Hypocrite! Like you've kept it in your pants for thirty /
years

MORT: In fact yes.

BEN: Bull / shit

MORT: Jewish boys make the best husbands. Everybody says.

BEN: Oh so what? You're excommunicating me now?

MORT: Excommun / icating?

BEN: You're eliminating me from the race—relig—*tribe*, whatever it is we are?

  . . .

Listen. We're nothing to each other, you and I. We're . . .
holiday-tolerant.
I grew up on Van Buren Street. You were on Kosciuszko.
Two blocks apart.

I have no memory of you.

When I was in the back room of your mother's "beauty parlor," I had no idea you were in the apartment upstairs.

We both went to movies at The Sumner.

So what?

How did it get us here?

What happened that made you hate me so much?

MORT: I don't give a crap about you, Benny, I never have.

You're okay.

You couldn't play stickball for shit but you were a little kid. Maybe you improved.

Anyway, it's in the past.

This is just business, Benny.

BEN: This is not how business is done.

MORT: Isn't it?

I thought it was.

BEN: . . . This is uni*magi*n / able

MORT: Again with the imagining.

You don't gotta imagine nothing, Benny.

Just *do*.

BEN: Morty, the thing is . . . this was a gift; it was a *gift* from my mother to my wife

. . . Let me give you *money* instead

MORT: Not interested.

BEN: It will exceed the value of this paste, this piece of *junk* that / you've set your

MORT: I do nicely

BEN: Oh yes, your career as a "fruiterer"?

I'm not even pur*su*ing it—

MORT: I make a nice living.

I got no complaints.

BEN: No complaints?

MORT: Uh-uh . . .

BEN *(Says it)*: Your entire life has been determined by a drunken fuck with a woman you didn't know and don't love and that led to a child you regret.

(Nothing Ben has said before has got to Mort; this stops him. He stares at Ben, almost trembling, angry and hurt and contemptuous. He looks as if he might do something, lunge, but he controls it. Pause.)

MORT: You don't understand shit, Benny. *(Decides to pretend to toss it off)*
    I don't mind.
    So what are you gonna do?

(Pause. Mort takes Polaroids out of his chest pocket, looks at them, puts them back.)

BEN: Your bidding.
MORT: . . . So *nu?*
BEN: . . . I'm going to my mother's hospital room. I'm going to spend some time alone with her.
MORT: Uh-huh.
BEN: While I'm there, she's going to have a sudden lucid spasm. During which she'll instruct me as to her wishes regarding the disposition of the "ruby necklace" she gave my wife to celebrate our engagement. So many years ago.
MORT: Very, very good.
BEN: I'm going to return home and report them.
    To Julie.
    And because she is impeccable—because she is *impeccable*, Mort—she's going to give me her blessing.
    So sweetly.
    And then I will hand over to you this piece of crap you so covet.
MORT: Very very good.
BEN: Yes.
MORT: When you gonna do it?
BEN: Tomorrow morning.

(Beat.)

MORT: When you gonna do it?

(Beat.)

BEN: Tonight.
> After the panettone . . . And the cognac.
> And before the demise.
> Presumably.
MORT: Good, Benny.
> Good boy.
JULIE *(Off, from a distance)*: Everybody get ready for dinner! /
FAYE *(Off, from a distance)*: And that's you, too, Mort!
> You better give me those Havanas. *(Ben hands them over)*
> They're illegal, you know.
> You're dealing in illegal cigars, Benny.
> You know what that is?

(Ben looks at Mort.)

Unimaginable to me.

A hallway. Jeff on the phone.

JEFF: No, we haven't eaten yet. They eat late.
> So where were you when I called before?
> Oh. What movie?
> Un-huh. No I didn't see—
> Uh-huh . . .
> So what did you do after?
> Oh.
> Un-huh.
> And how was
> Uh-huh. Their spare ribs have always been very hit-or-miss.
>
> . . .

Yeah it's great here.

It's incredible.

You would love the apartment, Mom—it's like the
sets of those plays you love.

With the "breezy dialogue."

They sort of *talk* that way and everybody's unbelievably
nice and, like, gracious and happy.

It's like you go to New York and you look for *New York*
but it isn't there? But it's *here* . . .

Maybe you will some day.

Maybe they'll invite you, who knows?

I'm the only non-blood relative, so

. . . Okay, I *know* how to behave you don't have to give
me tips in etiq—

They've already invited me for the summer!

They like me.

Yeah, they've got a place on *(He forgets where)*

The Vineyard.

Saltbox, very Hughdie Auchin

. . . Yes I told her.

I told her, Mom.

I'll tell her again to be sure.

You loved her in the movies especially in—uh-huh.

No. She *can't* come to the phone—

it's *chaos* here—*masses* of people.

Yeah—masses of blood relatives.

Yeah, like Catholics.

So. What?

Don't ask if you can ask just ask

. . .

I can't *believe* you're asking that.

I can't believe you're aski—

Why did I re*verse* the *charge*s?

Do you—

What?

do you begrudge me the dollar fif—

45

I can't fargin myself a phone call to my par
. . .
No, they didn't *ask* me to—I did this at my own—
Because it's the considerate

. . .
What?
That is so twisted.
That is such a tortuous—
No—they are *not* going to think that I think they're cheap.
They will *not* take this as an insult.
Maybe because they have developed beyond the ghetto mentality that has dominated you and destroyed any chance you—
Jesus. *Jesus*—
Why are you trying to make me—
Why do you want me to think I've *erred* . . .
Just because *you* might feel ill-at-ease at a place like—
Listen.
Do not attempt to inoculate me with your fucking first-generation diasporic insecuri—
No it is not pretentious—if you had ever
read a book or had an idea you would—
God! This is so fucking indicative!
You're so fucking *prim*itive! This is so fucking *typ*ical!
The way you *pounced* on the buffet table at graduation brunch I thought I'd
(Controlling himself.)
No I didn't bring that up *then* and I'm not

(He takes deep breaths.)

JULIE *(Off)*: Everybody get ready for dinner!
FAYE *(Off)*: And that's you, too, Mort!
JEFF: Listen
I've got to dress for dinner . . .

Yes. They do.

Because it's fucking *civilization* here.

Merry Christmas. Oh yeah right, I forgot, you're so *Orth*odox.

Joyous Tisha B'Av. *(Hangs up)*

Hallway/Timmy's room. Scotty pauses a moment. Timmy's in bed singing to himself. Scotty comes in.

SCOTTY: Timmy?

Timmy?

TIMMY: Scotty.

SCOTTY: Hey how do you feel, buddy?

TIMMY *(Mutters)*: Okay.

SCOTTY: You still got a fever? You still a little hot? *(Kisses his forehead)*

Not too bad.

Right, buddy?

You feeling a little better?

(Timmy nods.)

Good.

TIMMY: You eat yet, Scotty?

SCOTTY: Not yet.

TIMMY: What are you gonna eat?

SCOTTY: Oh now, I'm not gonna tell ya that, bud. 'Cause I don't want you to puke when I say we're having mm-mm and you picture it and you puke. You don't want *that* to happen, do you?

TIMMY: No.

SCOTTY: No . . . So you been okay when I was gone?

Till you got sick, I mean?

47

TIMMY: Yeah.

SCOTTY: 'Cause I missed you.

TIMMY: I missed you, too.

SCOTTY: Well, I hope so.

Because I would be devastated if that were not the case,
bud.

Absolutely de-*mol*ished.

TIMMY: I know.

SCOTTY: Yeah . . .

And Mommy and Daddy?

Have they been okay?

When I was gone?

(Timmy nods.)

Yeah?

Nothing oogly and disgooted about Mommy and Daddy
when I was gone?

(Timmy laughs.)

TIMMY: No.

SCOTTY: Okay.

Good.

Know what, babe?

You get better, I'm 'onna take you places.

TIMMY: Where?

SCOTTY: The Planetarium. With the stars, right?

An' it'll just be you an' me, okay?

None of the inglebroody and incrappitated people need
apply.

TIMMY: Yeah.

SCOTTY: Good.

JULIE *(Off)*: Everybody get ready for dinner!

FAYE *(Off)*: And that's you, too, Mort!

SCOTTY: That's me bud. I'm everybody.

TIMMY: But you're not *every* everybody.

SCOTTY: That's very true. And thank you for pointing it out.
I'm *not* every everybody.
I'm just the ma*jor*ity of everybody.
You go to sleep, okay?
I'll come look in on you later but you won't know it
'cause you'll be where the wild things are.

(He kisses Timmy on the forehead.)

Love ya, bud.

(Timmy grabs Scotty's head and kisses him on the forehead.)

TIMMY: You feel hot.

SCOTTY *(Smiling)*: Ya know what you are, kiddo?

TIMMY: What?

SCOTTY: A laff-riot. *(He starts off, looks back)* So everything's okay, right?

Part of the kitchen and part of the dining room.
Faye and Julie emerge from the kitchen with dishes.

JULIE: Come! Come and witness the immemorial scene:
Women Bearing Platters of Food!
Hurry before it's lost to the Mists of—oh!

(Scotty enters the dining room. Then Ben and Mort. Julie, having deposited her tray on the table, goes to Scotty.)

Sweetie, you're all sparkly! You look as if you've been bathing all day in waters fed by artesian—are you getting Timmy's flu? *(Because she's hugged him and put her hand to his forehead and he feels warm)*

SCOTTY: Not at all, Mom, don't / worry

JULIE: I worry— Is Ilana / coming?

SCOTTY: Probably not—we should start without her

JULIE *(Disappointed)*: Oh . . . I so wanted her to . . . Next year?

SCOTTY: Sure.

(Julie returns to fussing with the food.
    About Scotty in this scene: He has a social manner; it's not at all fake—it's disarmingly natural—but it is practiced and it lends him a quality both more solid and more starry than other young men.)

FAYE: Scotty!

SCOTTY: Aunt Faye.

FAYE: We haven't seen / you

SCOTTY: I'm sorry I've been so scarce.

FAYE *(Hugging him)*: Don't apologize. Would *I* be with us if I had another option?

SCOTTY *(Laughs)*: Auntie, you're hilarious. / You look great

BEN: Mort, rye bread's on the table straight from the freezer just the way you like it

MORT *(Reaches for it)*: Very good, very good

FAYE *(Slaps it out of his hand)*: You can *wait.*

SCOTTY: Hey, Uncle Mort

(Seeing Scotty, Ben is stricken.)

MORT: What's news, what's news?

SCOTTY *(Hugs Mort)*: Good to / see you

BEN *(Wants to stop the hug)*: Scott?

SCOTTY: Yeah, Dad?

BEN: . . . How are you?

SCOTTY: Good. How are you?

BEN: . . . Good. Fine.

(Shelley wanders in.)

SHELLEY: Hi!

SCOTTY: Shelley. *(He hugs her)* You look amazing

JULIE: Everybody take whatever seats you want; we're anarchists this year, no place cards

FAYE *(Overlaps)*: Shelley! Where were you?

SHELLEY: I don't know *where* I was—too many rooms in this house!

MORT: Shelley, sit down.

(Shelley sits.)

FAYE: So, Scotty? I heard you toured the Malaria Route.

SCOTTY: It was pretty rugged.

JULIE: I'm going to do one last inspection of the kitchen—you always think you've put out everything then it turns out you've forgotten the most expensive thing in the oven and you don't remember until it's a rancid odor

FAYE: I'll look with you, Julie.

BEN: No! I will!

FAYE: Forgive me for / living

BEN: You tame your family; kidding—

(Julie and Ben go to the kitchen. Julie does a look-round. Ben hangs back, looking at her.
Jeff enters the dining room. He's wearing a suit. Scotty sees him, bursts out laughing. Jeff blushes.)

JEFF: I . . .

SCOTTY: I didn't think you'd take me *seriously*.

(Jeff smiles crookedly.)

No, it's good, really.
    You look adorable
        . . . You'll get dates.

(People seat themselves, sort themselves out, Mort takes bread. Jeff looks wounded.
In the kitchen:)

JULIE: I think I actually got everything out there. First time! Isn't that unpreceden . . . Except the gravy spoon. *(She sees Ben looking at her)*
What are you looking at?
BEN: You.
JULIE: Have I come undone?
BEN: No. I still can't understand it

(Beat.)

JULIE: What?
BEN: Why you chose me
JULIE: Oh, are we in an abstracted and self-dramatizing mood and at the least convenient possible / time?
BEN: I mean it.
JULIE: My God, you had *so much money*!

(Beat.)

BEN: Except I didn't.
Not then.
JULIE: You're fishing.
BEN: I'm not.
I'm bewildered . . .
Sometimes I feel . . .
JULIE: . . . And sometimes you / don't
BEN: Nonexistent?
JULIE: I know.
BEN: You know?
You've sensed this in me?
JULIE: It's in Gail Sheehy.
BEN: You're mocking / me.

JULIE: I'm not mocking you, I'm dismissing you.
There's *din*ner.

(Beat.)

BEN: Listen, I have to tell you something.

(She listens. But he doesn't say anything.)

JULIE: Possibly . . . later . . . ? If . . . there's a . . . This isn't *real*,
is it?
BEN: . . . I
JULIE: Is there . . . something . . . specific?

(Beat.)

BEN: There are no specifics.

(Beat.)

JULIE: Because if there should be any . . .
I won't mind.

(Beat.)

BEN: That director, he heard your laugh, right? And he said to
himself: I must have questa ragazza for my next master-
piece di chinaymahtiko—
JULIE: Oh doll, *fairy* tales? / Now?
BEN: But this is true.
JULIE: Sometimes they *are*; still . . .
The goose will fly away if we / don't
BEN: You were at the automat.
JULIE: Twenty-One.
BEN: *Your* automat.
JULIE: You find *ways* to be right even if you're *absolutely* / wrong
BEN: And De Sica

JULIE: Not De Sica—can you at *least*, if you're going to gum up the works, get the *names* / right?

BEN: He heard you laugh before he even saw you— What were you laughing at?

JULIE: I don't re / member

BEN: . . . I *saw* you first. Cupid's dart

JULIE: Sweetie, you're making that up. I was famous.

The first time you saw me I was eighteen feet tall. *(He still stares at her)*

There are young men and Rappaports waiting for us; if we don't feed them, they'll start gnawing on each other . . . Later, maybe.

BEN: I'm going to go to the hospital later. See Mom.

JULIE *(Everything explained)*: Of course. I'll come with you.

BEN: No. I want to go alone.

JULIE: . . . Yes. That's best.

I'm so glad.

(She touches his face, kisses him. He smiles uncomfortably.)

Come.

(They return to the dining room. She looks at the table.)

Salt and pepper.

After all that self-congratulation, I forgot the salt and

JEFF: I'll get it with you!

JULIE *(Notices Jeff)*: Oh look at you!

Aren't you gorgeous!

You put the rest of us to shame!

Yes. Come help.

MORT: She needs help getting salt and pepper?

FAYE: Hush.

JULIE: How are your parents?

JEFF: Good. They say hi. *(Once they are in the kitchen, with some urgency)* He's not going to marry her.

JULIE *(Momentarily baffled)*: Sweetie?

JEFF: Scotty. He's not going to marry Ilana. In fact, they may be breaking up.

JULIE: Oh!

JEFF: But he doesn't want to go to Harvard next year. He thinks he may want to be a teacher. I'm trying to change his mind. *Please don't tell him I told you these things!*

JULIE: No . . . no.

JEFF *(Nods)*: Should I take the salt or the pepper?

JULIE: . . . The salt, I'd think.

(He takes it, returns to the dining room. She looks at him thoughtfully, then follows.

In the dining room there is a pleasant hubbub.)

Yes. Hello. Yes.

Everyone, it will delay eating even further, but I want to *say* something.

(They give her their attention.)

It's so lovely to be here

with all of you

with people I love and people I will love.

And mindful of people we love who are absent and in poor condition tonight—

well maybe not love . . . exactly . . .

But who are our own.

There are no real protocols here

but there's no reason not to make some up.

How I love formalisms. I've always thought God was bogus—do you like that, Scotty? "Bogus" like your generation

SCOTTY: Proud of you, Mom

JULIE: Anyway:

God is bogus and religion a scourge.

Still

I believe in something. Though I'm not sure what.
And I rather like prayer.
Prayer is
I think
yearning set to music!
And nothing is more human than to yearn.
Don't you agree, Jeff?

JEFF: Uh

JULIE: I know you do.
So lovely Christmas.
It's a pity, I guess, Ilana isn't here to
sort of legitimize us, though from what I understand
she's more pagan than Christian.
And anyway, it's a much purer matter of decor this
way, isn't it?
The holiness of shiny surfaces.
And you all look so shiny—
particularly the young ones!
All mystery—what will be? What will become of you?
But perhaps I'm digressing.
Oh I *did* want this to have some sort of structure.
Oh well, I suppose it's time to pass the platters and
oh! wait!
I thought of one other thing I like
and, yes, I think this will round out the toast
or prayer
or whatever this is
nicely.
I like
very much
the word "amen."
Does everybody know what that means?
It means:
I am in agreement.
Isn't that a lovely thought?
There are times I want to say amen to everybody—

the doormen and the greengrocer and even to Ben.
So I would love it if we would all just say it now
because I feel it's the case here among us all
and then we can eat.
All right? Count of three?
One—two—three—

ALL *(Generally, and some ambivalent)*: Amen.

JULIE: And now we can eat!

Act Two

Christmas Day, 2000

*The living room. It's gone slightly shabby.
Jeff is on the house phone.*

JEFF: Yes I know it's Christmas but the bathtub or the sink
　　　or the God forbid toilet in 15D does—
　　Uh-huh. Well, in addition this apartment itself is leak-
　ing from . . . I see.
　　Well what about young Mr. Figueroa? Diego?
　　*Car*los.
　　Right.
　　Right.
　　I'm sure, Mrs. Bascov would be happy to pay a Nativity . . .
　surcharge, if that . . .
　　Uh-huh—well—if you'd *ask*, I'd—
　　Thank you.
　　Feliz Navi—yeah. *(He hangs up)*
　　Julie?

JULIE *(Off)*: Yes?

JEFF: Maybe I can look under the sink.

Do you have a flashlight? Because the overhead / light is

JULIE *(Enters)*: I think the Y2K flashlight is in the escritoire.

JEFF: Okay.

JULIE: It's still in shrink-wrap so you'll have to tug.

JEFF: Oh—I'm never able to get those out.

Maybe I can see without seeing.

JULIE: Sweetie, I certainly didn't mean for you to become a janitor—

JEFF: No no, it's just the *immediacy* of a leak—

No plaster is falling at least

JULIE: Let it leak / then

JEFF: It's leaking at least into a *ba*sin

JULIE *(Simultaneous with above)*: It's leaking into a sink—I suppose we

JEFF: Damnable how no one will help simply because it's Christ / mas

JULIE: We always had to call the super for everything—Ben died still not knowing how to change a light bulb . . . I suppose I ought to find a pail or something and collect the water, what with scarcity scarcity everywhere

JEFF: Sure but— What would you do with the harvested wat—

JULIE: Flush the toilet with it? Isn't that what you do with harvested / water

JEFF: I think that's . . . hurricanes?

JULIE: Useless! I'm useless! I'm a dab hand at absolutely nothing! Comes the revolution I'm going to be thrown against a wall and shot down in my overcoat like the Ceauşescus—

JEFF: Surely / not

JULIE: It's the overcoats that break your heart, isn't it—even for the Ceauşescus who were despots—but, I mean, the dailiness of it, the trivial provision for comfort when you're going to be marched before a firing squad, it's piercing—

JEFF: Uh-huh, yeah.

Do you need help with dinner?

JULIE: No, dinner is perking away nicely on its own; boeuf bourguignon, how's *that* for a throwback?

JEFF: Because if you need *any* help don't be shy or—

JULIE: No no—you're being a dream—but I am *strong.*

JEFF: Then, I think I'll have at the valve—

JULIE: That's an excellent / idea

(Tim enters.)

TIM: Hey.

JULIE: Timothy! You're here!

Did we leave the front door unlocked? That's a / terribly careless thing to

TIM: No, I used my key.

JULIE: You haven't lost your key!

Oh, this really *does* feel like Christmas!

TIM *(Sees Jeff)*: Oh shit. Jeff man. *Shit.*

I didn't bring you a present

JEFF: That's completely not a / problem

TIM: But I brought my mom a present, I should have brought you

JEFF: That's very thoughtful of you / to bring your mom

TIM *(Thrusts a wrapped package at her)*: Here.

JULIE *(Hugs him)*: What gorgeous wrapping—let's put it under the tree. And I can spend all night trying to guess what it is.

That's my favorite part, the anticipation and the / specu

TIM *(To please her)*: It's a cookbook.

(Beat.)

JULIE: But there are scads of cuisines and I can sort of dream which / this might be and

TIM *(To please her some more)*: It's Mexican.

(Beat.)

JULIE: Thank you *so much*, sweetie, I'm

TIM: I'm really sorry, Jeff man, my mind is like all fractal geometry these days, I should have remem / bered

JEFF *(Goes to shake his hand)*: Tim, it's great to see you

TIM *(Hugs him)*: Yeah, you too, man. *(They nod)*

JEFF: I need to stem a leak; I'll see you / in a couple of minutes

TIM: Um, okay

JULIE: Come sit with me, sweetie

(Jeff exits.)

TIM: Um, yeah. Well . . . okay

(She leads him and they sit.)

JULIE: Baby?

TIM: Yes?

JULIE: You'll never guess whom I ran into last week.

TIM: Whom?

JULIE: Robman Glaspiegl.

TIM: Who's that?

JULIE: Well he's the president, darling.

TIM: Of the United States?

JULIE: Baby, of your college!

(Beat.)

TIM: Um I don't go to college?

JULIE: No but you did. For three and a half not entirely quixotic years. And last year, he took over the presidency. Anyway, we got to talking.

TIM: How?

JULIE: One does at these things.

TIM: What kind of thing / was it?

JULIE: It was a *charity* function—

TIM: Oh. What charity?

JULIE: I don't remember.

TIM: You don't remember?

Isn't that like the most important part?

JULIE: Something worthy.

All right?

Something worthy and wrenching and urgent and you get to dress up.

And anyway we got to talking—

TIM: How?

JULIE: We *fou*nd each other.

We were in proximity.

And we know each other.

TIM: How do you know / each other?

JULIE: We dated, all right?

TIM: You *dat*ed the president of my

JULIE: When we were fifteen. Don't be grossed out.

We didn't sleep together.

Anyway:

I acquainted him with your case

TIM: I don't have a case, Mom

JULIE: You *are a*—

Yes:

You *have* a case.

And Robman told me it would be in no way exceptional for a student in your posi

TIM: I'm not a / student

JULIE: Former student in your present position to complete his degree off-campus simply by writing his thesis while in consultation with an appropriate faculty member.

Not in any way exceptional.

You could make in-person office visits once or twice a semester. Which is not a hardship given that it's barely more than an hour away by train.

TIM: It's not like—what? Did you tell him I was an *English* major or something?

JULIE: They're people, / too

TIM: "Write your thesis on anthropogenic contaminants from the comfort of your home. Win cash prizes."

It doesn't *work* that way, Mom—

JULIE: I told him what your field is; he said it could all be managed—isn't that *great?*

(Tim looks fretful.)

TIM: I've got to go.

JULIE: Timothy.

TIM: I've got to go

JULIE: We can't keep skirting this, dear. You're simply not allowed to remain eternally amorphous. You're of too fine material for

TIM: I've got to / go

JULIE: Timothy

TIM: I've got to / go

JULIE: You mustn't be daunted, darling; there's nothing to be daunted by. According to the standardized tests, you're the brightest of any of us. If things were different, I might say all right, wealthy eccentric, glad tidings *go.*

But.

TIM: I'm very, like, promised forth?

JULIE: Where?

TIM: . . . Like everywhere?

JULIE: I don't ac*cept* that, sweetie.

"Everywhere" doesn't cut the mustard these days.

TIM: No it's—I have to work.

JULIE: Today?

TIM: Yeah.

JULIE: On Christmas?

TIM: I *know.*

JULIE: At the restaurant?

TIM: Yeah yeah I know—

It's . . .

Well, in a way it's enlightened because they, um,
mostly it's *Jews* who are working

JULIE: What?

TIM: And like *avowed* agnostics so they won't interfere with

JULIE: But that's

TIM: On the other hand awful I know 'cause it's like:

What is this, a roundup?

Are the trains waiting?

But maybe it's

inflammatory

to make that kind of comparison

JULIE: Sweetie?

TIM: Yeah Mom?

JULIE: The restaurant's closed today.

(Beat.)

TIM: . . . Did somebody just call?

JULIE: No, sweetie, I know how things like scheduling are not
your forte so I checked it out

TIM: You

JULIE: Checked it out

TIM: Holy

JULIE: yesterday

TIM: shit, holy shit

JULIE: just to make extra special sure we'd have you

TIM: This is

JULIE: and they told me they're closed

TIM: espionage?

JULIE: No—darling—

TIM: Jesus—you're like *Stasi.*

JULIE: Sweetie—

TIM: It's like the *sym*phony conductor ratting out the viola sec-
tion—

JULIE: I'm your mom.

(Beat.)

TIM: Oh oh—oh:
>To the *public*.
JULIE: Um?
TIM: You must have asked . . .
>Did you ask
>like
>for a reservation?

(Jeff reenters quietly, hangs back.)

JULIE: I just asked: Are you open on Christmas?
TIM: Well, there you are, that was your mistake.
>This is a private party.

(Beat.)

JULIE: *Is* it?
TIM: A family function—
>*"La famiglia."*
>And of *course* I tried to get out of it
>but
>I *need* this job
>and
>I'm
>Jewish.
>So.
JULIE: . . . I see.

(Pause. The pause lengthens.)

TIM: I can . . . take long breaks and shit.
JULIE: Can you?
TIM: I . . .
>yeah . . .
>it's Christmas.
>What are they gonna do: Fire me?

JULIE: I'd say not.

(The doorbell rings.)

Faye! That must be—
JEFF: I'll get it for you—
JULIE: Nononono.
    I'm *strong*

(And she's off. A moment. Tim just stands there. Jeff approaches.)

JEFF: Look, it's not my place but you've got to cut this shit.
TIM: What shit?
    There's no shit to
JEFF: Your mother.
    You have to be here.
TIM: . . . I'm
    here,
    I—
    What do you mean?
JEFF: Tim.

(Pause.)

TIM: Okay.
    Like: first:
    We don't *know* she's
JEFF: We do.

(Beat.)

TIM: This is a complicated *time* in my
JEFF: All times are complicated
TIM: This is more?
JEFF: It doesn't matter.

TIM: . . . Molly is, like

JEFF: It makes no difference

TIM: Jeff man, whoa, okay?

　　There are competing imperatives involved—

JEFF: Oh guess what: The competition has ended, your mom
　　has won.

(Faye and Julie enter. Faye with bags.)

FAYE: Hello Hello Hello Hello!

(From the boys: ad-lib greetings.)

　　Jeff, so nice to see you. You look wonderful. You've gained
　　a little *gravi*tas.

(Jeff goes to her. She kisses him.)

JEFF: And you, Faye.

FAYE *(Referring to Tim)*: Uh!

　　Heart-stopper!

　　Come here.

*(Tim goes to her. A little shyly; he likes her. She smooches
him.)*

　　Look at you—*look* at you!

TIM: Merry Christmas, Aunt / Faye—damn! I didn't *get* you any

FAYE *(Staring at his face)*: It's uncanny.

　　Julie, it's uncanny—

　　You'd think over time it would lessen . . .

(Awkward pause.)

JULIE *(Brightening)*: What have you brought?

FAYE: I'm late because Pathmark didn't have a babka.

　　Do you believe it?

JULIE: No babka!

FAYE: I know: This day, sans babka. I am persona non grata—
Finally, I found a simulacrum at a Korean deli. I won't
vouch for it but at least it's a gesture in the direction. And
I brought those curtains / I told you about

JULIE: All the way from / Roslyn?

FAYE: I shlepped them on the LIRR, it was good, I didn't have
to sit next to anybody. I'm dying to see if they work in the
bedroom, we can just hold them up, we don't have to / hang
them

JULIE: Let's go then

FAYE: First I need to visit the bathroom—

JULIE: Main one's kaput. You'll need to use the one in the sitting room— I'll take you there, you'll never / find it.

FAYE: After all these years . . . it's true.

JULIE: Hilarious—oh! All these glamorous entrances and
exits—I've missed them!

*(Julie and Faye head off. Jeff and Tim are left with their
conversation.)*

JEFF: I don't mean to overstep.

TIM: Jeff man—I just don't want you to be burdened, okay?

JEFF: I'm not.

TIM: I really appreciate how you've always like
maintained this presence in my life.

JEFF: I only

TIM: Like always remembering my birthday and presents
and the letters, that was really nice and I'm *so contrite*
that I forgot to get you / anything

JEFF: That's not a

TIM *(Continuous)*: And I know that you were kind of like trying to be this ersatz big brother to me. Like to kind of
substitute for Scotty and all?

JEFF: I would never presume to do that.
I know I could never . . . play that role.

TIM: Right: You can't

JEFF: Yes, I realize

TIM: 'Cause I don't remember him . . .

I don't remember the guy.

He's like: The Family Myth.

(Beat.)

So you shouldn't feel like you need to re-cre*ate* something . . .

'Cause there's nothing. Okay?

You can be, like, Trusty Family Friend Jeff Who's Always There For Us And Of Whom We're Fond.

(Beat.)

Which should prove less *bur*densome to you

JEFF: You don't remember him?

TIM: I think

he was . . . nice.

He was nice, right?

JEFF: Yes.

TIM: I remember someone being nice to me

. . .

I mean

they *tried* but my mom is not one of your more *factual* people.

She'd just say, "Oh Scotty," or some shit like that and she'd get this look.

And my dad, he was like,

"Oh Scott Scott," and there'd be all these tales of der-ring-do

and prognostications of what would have been

and what the world had lost and I'd listen and be like: Okay, this is not people.

But I guess it was nice for him to think so?

. . .

And you know once Scotty got bad-sick they wouldn't
let me near him?
Like they were afraid I'd catch it?
Or, I think, he looked bad.

JEFF: Yes.

TIM: Yeah, I think he looked really, really bad.
They didn't want to scare me
And I was only five or something prenatal like
that so really what do you expect?

(Beat.)

JEFF: In that case, with my authority as the trusty family friend
on whom you can rely, I tell you, you must hang around here.
All the time, Tim.

(Beat.)

TIM: It's not like I don't love my / mom— Jeez—

JEFF: No one is saying / that

TIM: Molly kinda needs me around, too—

JEFF: Bring her here.

TIM: I can't

JEFF: There are plenty of rooms—drafty and with leaks, and
you'll get chilblains / but

TIM: I can't bring her here.

JEFF: You can.
You *will.*

TIM: Right. *(Beat)* Okay. *(Beat)* Right.
The thing is

(Pause. Big decision.)

Molly is, like . . . in a vague way . . . knocked up?

(Beat.)

JEFF: Shit. *(Beat)* You don't use a

TIM: Not that time, no

JEFF: The point is to use it every / time

TIM: Nobody uses it every time when they're going out with / one

JEFF: I beg to differ

TIM: Maybe *you* do. But then, you've always struck me as
an exceptionally *ruly* sort of fellow, Jeff.

But other than you, *no.*

JEFF: —Well, I'm not going to comment on that chipper bit
of sociology.

So. Jesus!

Is she going to *have* it?

Is she going to *have* this preventable white child?

TIM: We can't, like, decide?

We've been pretty feckless about it, to be completely
truthful.

Truthfully, we've been in*ord*inately feckless. We just go
back and forth.

JEFF: May I put in my two cents?

TIM: I'd very much appreciate them.

JEFF: You're extremely young.

You don't have prospects.

You barely have a job.

Who knows if this relationship has a future? A baby
will yoke you forever.

Looked at common-sensically . . . it's a bad idea, Tim.

TIM *(Nods)*: I appreciate that, Jeff.

That strikes me as very lucid thinking. As I would only
expect from you

. . .

The only thing is? She's in her eighth month?

JEFF: Oh fuck.

TIM: So I mean . . . like . . .

that decides it, right?

'Cause the alternative is . . . gruesome

. . .

So, I mean, she can't be here.

'Cause my mom will not fail to *note* and correctly in*ter*-pret the obstetric mass

JEFF: Tim, eventually your mom is going to

TIM: Well . . . not necessarily.

Right?

(Beat.)

Like I think, in the far reaches of the night, my mom derives *great comfort* from saying to herself, Well, at least he hasn't im*preg*nated anyone. And I don't want to take that away from her.

JEFF: You're not a fuck-up.

TIM: I'm pretty feckless, Jeff, I'm pretty goddamn feck—

JEFF: You're young.

TIM: I'm not that / young.

JEFF: Christ, of course / you

TIM: You just like to think people are young so that you can still be young but: I'm not that young

JEFF: . . . How do you intend to sup*port* this child?

TIM: Shit if I know.

Sell my body?

JEFF: Tim.

TIM: I don't *mean* it, Jeff . . .

That's totally a last resort.

JEFF: Oy. This *secrecy*—it isn't a plausible strategy

TIM: Jeff man, you gotta keep this to yourself,

you *pro*mised.

JEFF: When was that?

TIM: Come *on.*

Really.

(Beat.)

You're like a *brother* to me—

(Julie enters with a platter.)

JULIE: The quest for the babka has outflanked Faye; she's lying down. You're still here!

TIM: I'm going.

JULIE *(Setting down the platter)*: I've brought gougères *(Going to liquor cart)*

 The curtains look very promising by the—
 What are we drinking?

TIM: I'm gonna see you later, Mom.

JULIE: *Will* you?

TIM *(Unconvincing)*: Yeah.

JEFF *(Jovial)*: Of course you will.

 (Undertone, blackmail) You'll want to be checking up on me.

(Tim's eyes widen.)

TIM: Later, Mom

JULIE: Yes . . . yes.

(Tim goes. She has a faltering moment.)

Scotch?

 I have this lovely scotch, it's very peaty, very smoky, it will remind you of your favorite day in fall, you'll drink it neat.

JEFF: Yes, thank you.

(She brings drinks, sits.)

JULIE: I frighten him.

JEFF: I don't think it's that

JULIE: He thinks of me as a sort of special effect from a horror movie. Fast-forward, the flesh falls off and nothing left but the howling skeleton, something like that.

 You don't want to terrify your child.

JEFF: I'm sure that isn't

JULIE: He runs away.

He won't look at me. He never looks at me.

(Jeff can't speak to this.)

He's so unfinished.

I still have so much to do to him.

I don't know if . . .

(She lives in this a moment, shakes it off. Brightly:)

I'll get to it when I get to it and it will be fine!

Let's be a drinks party, you and I. I'm so happy to have you back.

JEFF: I'm so happy to / be here

JULIE: I never realized how much I'd counted on being able to see you until you were gone.

Oh! And thank you for having a look into my finances such as they / are.

JEFF: Not at all

JULIE: Things have got a little out of hand what with one thing and / another

JEFF: I'm glad I can / help

JULIE: We need to talk about / payment

JEFF: I won't hear of it

JULIE: But

JEFF: Shut up.

Shut up.

(A moment.)

JULIE: Five years in Chicago!— What could you have been thinking?

Have a gougère, by the— *(He takes one)*

Did you love it?

The Midwest!

Did you make tons of money?

JEFF: Yes.

To the money.

This gougère is

JULIE: Oh good!

I like to imagine a great flock of money dive-bombing you like a Hitchcock scene.

But how could you stand it?

JEFF: Well

JULIE: And why did you go?

I'll pause so you can answer.

JEFF: . . .

Chicago seemed . . . plausible.

It's a city, there are Jews, the office was exciting, the deal I negotiated staggering.

They wanted me.

And New York had been . . . for a while . . .

JULIE: *Did* you like it there?

JEFF: For a time, yes.

Very much.

I did well

. . .

There was a case, it was sort of thorny—we had to decide whether to litigate or settle.

The decision was up to me.

The thing was, the award was potentially gigantic but a misstep would have been disastrous.

I had a number of meetings with the head of the department, *many* I suppose.

The discussions were quite sane, I thought, quite precise, it was even exhilarating in a way, Socratic.

Then out of the blue, he screamed at me, "Fucker, you say 'on the one hand' one more time, you're only gonna *have* one hand."

. . .

That sort of signaled that my time there had drawn to a close.

JULIE: I see

  . . .

And what about the woman?

JEFF: Woman?

JULIE: Wasn't there a woman?

JEFF: No

  . . .

Not really, no

  . . .

She was married and . . . I respect people's vows

  . . .

I would sort of *gawk* at her? I think?

  . . .

I took to asking her weirdly neutral questions.
She'd say things like: "How would *I* know the proportion of water to rice? I can't cook toast."

  . . .

Eventually, she darted into rooms whenever I'd . . . pass

  . . .

Sort of hilarious, if you think about it.
I've tried very hard . . . to do the right thing.
To be . . . fair? Even?
Apparently, that's an outrage, people *blame* you for it.
It's tiring. Rather: "World Without Amen, End," do you know?
So . . . I decided it was time for a break.
And I came back.
Home.

JULIE: But you're staying at one of those awful corporate high / rises

JEFF: Just for the time being.

Anyway, I have *this* place.

(A moment. It gets itchy.)

So boeuf bourguignon and . . . ?

JULIE: Oh!

It's a mad menu, you'll go crazy for it!

We start with clear soup

JEFF: Clear soup, like / the old plays

JULIE: Then quenelles Escoffier.

Then the stew.

And with the stew I'm making popovers

JEFF: I love pop / overs

JULIE: Sort of a Yorkshire pudding idea.

And petits pois. And lyonnaise potatoes

JEFF: Wow

JULIE: I know: Insane, yes?

For four people, two of them old ladies good for
a forkful a piece.

. . .

I *hope* four people.

JEFF: It will be.

JULIE: He prefers . . . the company of others, these days.

His *girl*friend

JEFF: Do you know her?

JULIE: I met her once.

JEFF: And is

JULIE: Lovely, oh, lovely!

She looked as if she'd chosen her clothes in 1978 and
never put them up for review—

this floor-length kind of peasant burlap thing—it was
*touch*ing.

And there was a *recorder* sticking out of her backpack—
I was terrified there was going to be an outbreak of
"Greensleeves" but . . . there wasn't.

She's . . . timeless, I think.

He likes her.

He has a way of . . . no longer showing up here.

He passes through.

He doesn't even visit, he . . . tithes to his conscience.

If he would just give me . . . one whole evening.

JEFF: He will tonight.

JULIE: Will he?

> You guarantee it?

JEFF: I do: Scotty will be back.

JULIE: Scotty?

(Beat.)

JEFF *(Mortified)*: I'm so sorry

JULIE: That's

JEFF: God, I can't believe I

JULIE: Jeff!

> Believe it or not, I remember that I had a son named
> Scott.
>
> You haven't done anything wrong
>
> . . .
>
> You think of him sometimes.

JEFF: . . . Sure. Of course.

> Sometimes
> when I see someone
> you know
> "in public life,"
> a judge or senator even
> someone our age
> and already distinguished
> I'll think—and be absolutely certain—
> That would have been Scott.
> Do you ever do that?

JULIE: I don't.

> He really didn't have all that much potential.

(Jeff looks at her.)

> People have their seasons and Scotty's was extreme youth.
> He lacked some kind of focus. That drop of
> ruthlessness.

He would have had a fine life, a very happy life,
but he would have disappointed some people.
His father. Oh Ben would have been crushed,
I think— But then he was himself so very . . .
. . .
I had this idea *you* were the one.

JEFF: . . . I don't know what that means.

JULIE: You see this so often, don't you?

Pairs of young people.

And one is all feathered and aglow and the other . . .
hangs back.

But you get that one alone . . . and there's a sort of
sneak stardom . . . and a cunning . . . that you can glean
if you know how these things go.

And in time the peacock fades and the one in the shad-
ows shines and you tell people of their beginnings and
everyone is so surprised: Really, they thought that mild
guy was it and this one not so much?

There was this moment . . . I thought that was you and
Scotty.

I thought you would . . . flourish.

JEFF: Really?

JULIE: Yes.

I saw the most dazzling life for you.

JEFF: My God.

(Beat.)

JULIE: What happened?

*(Jeff thinks about this. When he speaks, it's not an evasion
but the factual and complete answer, delivered plainly.)*

JEFF: Nothing happened.

(Julie takes him in.)

JULIE: What am I going to do with you?

JEFF *(Agreeably)*: I know. I know. I'm impossible!

JULIE: Jeff.

JEFF: Yes?

JULIE: That was not a rhetorical question.

(Faye enters.)

FAYE: I am such an old woman. I can't think what it is.

JULIE: No luck napping?

FAYE: No: I keep trying to remember

JULIE: Vodka?

FAYE: Yes, sweetie, thanks.

(Julie goes to get it.)

What is missing from this apartment? I cannot figure it out.

JULIE: Vigor? Promise? Fresh paint? Functional plumbing?

FAYE: But what *else*?

JULIE *(Hands her the drink)*: I don't know.

FAYE: Ugh! It's driving me crazy.

    I—

    Timmy? What's / up with him?

JULIE: He had to go to the restaurant. It's Christmas so they're
only working Jews and agnostics.

FAYE: . . . I'll let that pass without comment.

    I assume you've all been discussing how democracy in
this country is now at its lowest ebb in our lifetime.

JULIE: Yes. And stew.

FAYE: Mm, this cheese puff is supernal.

    Do you believe this new idiot? Is he depressing? I mean,
the President of the United States?

    I'm starting to get nostalgic for his father. Who always
felt to me like middle management in a fluffernutter fac-
tory but I *mean*. What a way to start a century!

JEFF: Yes

JULIE *(Simultaneous with above)*: Well

FAYE: "Who's the Prime Minister of India?" they ask him.

"Jeepers, let me look that up!"

The Prime Minister of India!

That's not Postmaster General of Trinidad-Tobago.

I have never in my life been so grateful that politics mean nothing to me.

Remember how Bernice and Moishe used to get?

JULIE: I *feel* as though I do.

FAYE: Ugh: senile! You never met Bernice and

JEFF: They were your sister and

FAYE: Yeah. The ones who died young.

The ones who died ex*treme*ly young.

JEFF: Commies?

FAYE: Fanatics.

JEFF: I like to read about those thirties' street-corner pamphleteers.

FAYE: It makes great reading. Living with it!

I remember Friday night dinner where they wouldn't hand each other the chicken because one's a Trotskyist, one's a Leninist and how can you pass chicken across such a divide? . . . As if that was going to be the issue for eternity there on Van Buren Street.

Funny though.

That's all disappeared from the family. Without a trace.

JEFF: I think Scott had some of

FAYE: Oh right, didn't he used to hold up signs with that meshuggenah girlfriend of his? What was her name? / Devora?

JULIE: I don't remember her name.

JEFF: Ilana

JULIE: Yes.

FAYE: That wasn't the same thing, trust me.

Nostalgia.

A waste of time.

It's the *future* that matters.

(Pause. A bit melancholy. It worsens. The phone rings.)

JULIE: Oh good! We needed the phone to ring just then. *(As she goes to it:)* A few seconds earlier would have been even better.

FAYE *(Something of an undertone)*: Are you being her chargé d'affaires?

JEFF: To a degree: *start*ing to.

FAYE: We'll talk.

JULIE *(Referring to the phone ID)*: Oh good.

Oh I'm *so* delighted.

Faye, you're going to be very glad you're awake!

FAYE: What's she done?

JULIE *(On phone)*: Sweetie?

Oh, sweetie, I'm so glad you called back.

Wait a minute, I'm gonna put you on speaker. *(Does so)*

Your mother's here.

FAYE: Oh Jesus, oh God

JULIE: And you remember our friend Jeff Bornstein.

JEFF: Hi, Shelley.

SHELLEY *(Simultaneous with above)*: I don't know nobody named Jeff Bornstein.

FAYE *(Undertone)*: I don't know *any*body named Jeff / Bornstein.

JEFF: She does / though

JULIE *(To Faye)*: I did this. I hope it's

SHELLEY: Aunt Julie?

JULIE: *Yes*, sweetie?

(From the speaker, in the background: a man speaking Spanish.)

JEFF: Who's that?

FAYE: Don't ask.

SHELLEY: How did you get my number?

JULIE: Well, I—I just *have* it; you're listed

SHELLEY: Why are you calling me?

JULIE: Oh! Well—to wish you a Merry Christmas and because
  I simply thought:
  Enough of this *non*sense
  this . . .
  incommunicado between you and your mother.
  And it's the holidays and it seemed absurd
  to let this meaningless es*trang*ement continue

SHELLEY: *Stop butting into everybody's business!*
  This is none of your business!
  You're always trying to make people do what you want
  them to do!

FAYE: Shelley!
  This is Mom—shut up!

SHELLEY: You don't even *like* me!
  You *never* liked me!
  You always made *fun* of me!

JULIE: That isn't so— Who? Which one of us do you mean,
  darling?

FAYE: *Both.* She means *both.*
  I'm going to have a break / down

JULIE: I'm—so—sorry—

FAYE: I wish I were still on Digilene, / I swear it

SHELLEY: *You think you're so special because you were in the*
  movies!
  You think you're the boss of us

FAYE: Shelley—stop this at once!

SHELLEY: Stop *calling me*, Aunt Julie!
  You run out my tape!
  I need my tape for my potholder orders!
  Stop thinking you're special!
  I know nobody ever wanted me at the holidays!
  You just dragged me along like garbage in a suitcase.

JULIE: None of this is *true*, of *course* we / wanted

SHELLEY: I gotta sell potholders!
  Stop running out my tape!

Stop calling me!
I'm a grown-up!
I don't gotta talk to you no more!

(Someone wrests the phone from Shelley. Hector speaks:)

HECTOR: *Que se larguen todos a la mierda . . . déjenla quieta . . .*
¡¡Coño, que se vayan al carajo!! (A little confusion as they try
to hang up) ¿Bueno, hemos acabado?
SHELLEY *(Crying):* *¿Hector, por qué no me dejan quieta? Que*
tengo . . .
HECTOR: They'll leave you, they'll leave you. Hang up,
      Shelley, hang

(And they hang up. Long silence.)

JULIE: She really has become quite independent, hasn't she?
FAYE: This is excessive.
      I understand resentment.
      But this is more than her share.
      I made mistakes but only to an ex*tent.*
      No, I won't *have* this, I refuse.
JULIE: I'm so terribly sorry

(Faye goes to the phone, dials. It's still on speaker. We hear:
"If you wanna order a potholder, leave your name and
address and phone number after the noise.")

FAYE: Shelley? So nu, you're not picking up?
      Fine.
      Shelley, what a monster,
      what a little dybbuk you've become.
      Listen, thank God you never had children
      but if you had, you would know that to err is
      parenthood and I was within the requisite limits.
      We're all resenters but your portion is excessive.

You were always like this.

You always helped yourself to too much; you
think you were so easy?

You were a shonda at every holiday with the potatoes!
If we never speak again and you don't hear from me
till I'm dead rest assured *that's* not what killed me.
Good-bye and ganug.

HECTOR *(His voice picking up)*: *Carajo,*

FAYE: And screw you, too, you Puerto Rican prick. *(Hangs up.
Breathes heavily)* I'm not a prejudiced woman but racial
slurs come in handy at times of high emotion.

(Beat.)

JULIE: 718.

So is it Brooklyn

or Queens that she's

FAYE: Brooklyn.

JULIE: I see. Do you know what neighbor / hood

FAYE: One of them.

I don't give a damn.

Gei gesundheit.

JULIE: I wanted to make you a little treat.

FAYE: I know, sweetie.

You always think the best of everyone.

It's not useful, sweetie.

JULIE: Forgive me.

FAYE: No, sweetie, no.

Your intentions were delightful.

. . .

I'm going to try that nap again, I think.

It's rude but I plead old age.

JULIE: All right, yes, good idea.

FAYE: Wake me if . . . you're afraid I've *perished* or something.

(Julie and Jeff alone.)

JEFF: It . . . was a delightful . . . attempt.

JULIE: I really don't have time to be this incompetent.

My learning curve . . . can't even *curve* really.

I have too much to do

. . .

Well. I'll just develop the skills I need and that's all there is to it!

I'm checking on the dinner in all its absurd abundance.

JEFF: May I help you?

JULIE: No.

(Softening) Give me a little while.

You can . . . amuse yourself, yes?

Of course you can.

It must be what you do.

(She walks off, leaving him alone.
Fade.)

Some terrible drone of a tired Christmas classic.
It runs down like a failing battery.
Lights: Jeff alone on his cell phone.

JEFF: Tim, if you're there, pick up. Oh shit, you're not there.

Listen—I understand your situation—I get the "imperatives" here—I really do—but you can *spare* the *evening*.

Nothing will happen—and if it does—it's not as if you're living in an oasis-less desert or something—assistance is available—everywhere.

You have to come.

You have to.

You can't imagine . . . how much it—

You don't have a choice, it's the only thing to do.

And Tim? When I tell you, "You don't have a choice,"

I advise you to remember there are things I could *say*.

I'm ... a time-bomb here. *(Hangs up)*

Even I don't believe that.

(Jeff has been decorating the Christmas tree, returns to it. Faye enters.)

FAYE: Where's Julie?

JEFF: *Her* turn to nap.

She checked on the dinner; it made her tired.

Things do now.

FAYE: Ah. What *is* dinner, anyway?

JEFF: Boeuf bourguignon.

Very well *done* boeuf bourguignon.

And many accompaniments.

I'm hungry.

FAYE: So much food, so little eating.

Timmy's not yet

JEFF: He's still ...

FAYE: at work with the other Jews and agnostics?

JEFF: Yes.

FAYE: What is that? Bistro apartheid?

You don't believe that story, do you?

JEFF: Why not?

FAYE: How I adore that little boy. But he's twenty-four years old and calling him "little boy" is not a conceit.

What's going to be with him?

He'll be all alone.

JEFF: It would seem so, wouldn't it?

FAYE: I don't wanna think about it.

Let me help with that. *(She joins him decorating)*

By the way, I was an excellent mother.

JEFF: I'm sure.

FAYE: I was a dedicated and loving mother. And believe me, it wasn't easy because Shelley was such a lump.

This "I hate you" was something she decided one day.

Her version of a career choice.

You never know.

JEFF: No.

FAYE: There's no predicting.

Look at Scotty.

Straight. Never took a drug. Who'd think he's gonna end up an AIDS victim?

JEFF: They don't like when you call them victims.

FAYE: Who'd think he's gonna end up an AIDS *beneficiary*?

JEFF: I take your point.

FAYE: "He's caught Timmy's cold, oh it's not Timmy's cold, it's some weird bug he picked up in his travels—don't worry, he's in New York City now, we'll take care of it."

Do yourself a favor: Never have a blood transfusion in 1981.

JEFF: If I can possibly avoid it

FAYE: Even the *good* kids.

You haven't broadcast your seed, have you? No little illegitimates dotting the land?

JEFF: No.

FAYE: Smart thinking: I salute you.

And your parents? How are

JEFF: They've moved south.

FAYE: South?

JEFF: Yes.

FAYE: You mean like Boca?

(Jeff blushes.)

HA!

You must find that very embarrassing.

Listen: Ignore them.

JEFF: I do . . .

FAYE: Is it me or does this tree get uglier with every piece of struhlkes we hang on it?

JEFF: It's *most* hideous.

(They pause, then continue.)

FAYE: My goal for this party was *Meet Me in St. Louis,* I think
  we're falling short.
JEFF: Mm-*hm.*
FAYE *(Quits):* Ach. *(As she gets a vodka)* So you're in charge here?
JEFF: I'm . . . helping out.
FAYE: There's no other place you need to be this Christmas?
JEFF: Not my holiday, really . . .

  Even if it *were* . . .
FAYE: I see.

  So what's next for you?
  Are you ditching the corporate law thing and becoming,
  I don't know, *good?*
  Setting up some storefront—
JEFF: I'm not a lawyer anymore.
FAYE: . . . Disbarred? Interesting.
JEFF: I'm in good standing in both New York and Illinois
FAYE: Then
JEFF: I *am* not working as a lawyer now; I *will* not be working
  as a lawyer again; therefore: I'm not a lawyer . . .
  What about you?
FAYE: Me? I'm a merry widow.
JEFF: *Are* you merry?
FAYE: I'm okay.

  I have my house, my . . . pursuits.
  Lively friendships with a small group of un-husbanded
  ladies; it's not much to have in common but we pretend.
JEFF: Do you miss Mr.—
FAYE: It's surprising how that happens.
JEFF: . . . Sorry.
FAYE: No it's good.

  So.

  If you're not to be a lawyer . . . what are you to be?
JEFF: Oh! *(Then his voice sounds a little far away)* There are so
  many possibilities.

(He at last gives up on the tree.)

May I ask you something about Ben?

FAYE: Go. Ask.

JEFF: There were some rumors

FAYE: They're all true.

JEFF: You *know* this?

FAYE: In my heart-of-hearts.

JEFF: That would make him, of course, a criminal.

FAYE: Listen, he modeled himself on Joseph P. Kennedy; why leave that part out?

JEFF: . . . And did he manage somehow to pay an enormous penalty to avoid going to jail?

FAYE: So I've always believed

JEFF: Because there's nothing left.

FAYE: . . . Yes.

JEFF: How could he have allowed that

FAYE: For convenience sake, we say that after Scotty died, he lost his bearings . . .

JEFF: *Did* he?

FAYE: Why not?

JEFF: But . . . *did* he?

FAYE: He was my brother; I really didn't know him very well.

JEFF: I had no idea—I mean, I was *astonished* to discover that they were renters—this seemed to me the antithesis of a rental—I thought it was a fortress!

FAYE: Yes.

JEFF: Before there was, it seemed, some leeway, some sympathy and even humanity, but the new owners are not inclined that way

FAYE: Why would they / be?

JEFF: There's been an exorbitant offer on the apartment downstairs but it's contingent on their being able to buy *this* place, too—apparently fourteen rooms is not enough for three people, they're looking to form, I don't know, the nucleus of a *king*dom or something. And there's only so

much negotiating and stalling to counter the horrid tricks
buildings play to rid themselves of undesired tenants

FAYE: Sure

JEFF: And the thought that that would be . . . her . . .

FAYE: Ending

JEFF: . . . is, I think, unbearable.

FAYE: Yes

JEFF: . . . None of this is new to you.

FAYE: Who do you think was you during the last hospitalization?

(Jeff looks at her.)

I'm the remnant, kiddo.

JEFF: It's an impossible situation.

FAYE: Is it?

JEFF: I'd pay for it myself, except she'd never accept charity.
I've thought of funneling the money into her account
without telling her.
But . . . somehow . . . that's disrespectful.

FAYE: Ah.

*(Julie enters with a tray of mugs. She is wearing a gorgeous
vintage gown from the forties.)*

JULIE: I've brought consommé!

FAYE: Julie!

JEFF: Look at you!

JULIE: I've brought it in mugs so it's not an actual course—this
way we're not actually starting—we're just having a little
liquid nibble before our company's assembled.

(They take mugs. She has brought four. She looks up:)

Is that—?
Oh.
I thought I heard . . .

Well, I didn't so I didn't!

Have you tried the soup?

Isn't it good?

JEFF: De / licious.

FAYE: Lovely.

JULIE: It's my mother's recipe.

*Ev*erything is in it.

You start by roasting bones.

There was a moment—looking at the bones laid out on the tray—but then

I just got over it!

JEFF *(To brighten)*: She cooked, too, your mother?

JULIE: Oh yes. Yes!

She was ob*sessed* with food. She wrote about food and read about food and cooked food and dreamed food. She did everything you could do with food short of eating it, which she didn't do once in the thirty-seven years I knew her.

FAYE: And that's her dress you're wearing, of course.

JULIE: Yes. Do you like it?

FAYE: Very beautiful.

JEFF: Incredible, really.

FAYE: But I love all her dresses.

JULIE: I have a trunkful of them. I'm going to wear every one once before I . . . Oh yes, she had an exquisite sense of line and volume and drape.

And you take the dresses apart and see the bones and she was—Palladio!

She was Christopher Wren. Genius.

She made scrawny women look voluptuous and fat women look voluptuous.

Sex was her métier. Professionally. Privately . . . less so. *(She laughs)*

How do I look? Dare I ask?

JEFF: Voluptuous.

JULIE: I'm going to be Irish now and say: Lord love you for a liar.

JEFF: Only I'm not lying.

> You look incredibly beautiful.

(Julie is halted by this. They smile at each other.)

JULIE *(Almost inaudible)*: Thank you

> . . .

> Jenny's dresses, they do that for a girl!

FAYE: It isn't / the dress

JEFF: Was she a good mother?

FAYE: Bite your tongue!

> That's no kind of question.

JULIE: No, it's all right.

> She wasn't like Rivka, she wasn't an enemy.

> She was . . . neither this nor that! She had so much to cope with, my father walking out on us so suddenly and so early.

> She was certainly not the sort who cripples you

> and haunts you and whom you blame even when

> you're old and wizened . . . or as wizened as you get to get.

> On the other hand, when she died . . . it wasn't as though the gap . . . could

> never be filled. *(She becomes thoughtful now, goes away, abruptly brings herself back)*

> She was as good to me as she could afford to be and that's all you can ask.

FAYE: Amen to that.

JULIE: This was my favorite of her dresses because I watched her make it.

FAYE: *Did* you?

JULIE: Yes!

> She had a sewing machine in the apartment.

> In a closet of a room off the kitchen, I think it had started out as a spare pantry.

> But she'd installed this fearsome old Singer from the Year One, you know the kind?

With the angry bobbin and the rusty treadle, black and glowering.

It was—I think—the one her father had bought her when she was sixteen and he'd figured out who she was and managed to scrape together the pennies for it and presented it to her with . . . such pride!

Though it was hideously ugly in the apartment.

And—my God!—why a sewing machine anyway? When there were factories here and abroad executing in intricate detail her every notion . . .

But some nights, she would sneak down to this tiny room and . . . work the machine.

And this one time—just once because I wouldn't risk it—I sneaked down after her. And I hid myself and watched . . .

I barely recognized her. She wasn't . . . fretful. The way she was with me. She wasn't inadequate.

That was gone.

She was gone.

She had become . . . allegorical:

Woman at the Loom.

Such gorgeous nimble obliviousness.

I was silenter than silent.

I didn't want anything, least of all me, to interfere with the . . .

loving-kindness of her attention.

Oh I loved her. That woman. Who had been my mother.

. . .

I think
somehow
that's what she deeded to me.
Not the genius, of course,
or the concentration,
but,
oh what am I saying?

. . .

I look around me, I know it's dilapidation
but I *love* it:
It's the memories that erode the things, after all,
and the things . . . in themselves—
I'm saying this badly

. . .

This dress: it's the record of an intention
and—the joy of that!—
And each tiny dwindling object in the room—is historical!
And the decay only means it's still alive.
And even after . . . the cruelest losses, savage, unsurvivable losses, there came a day when
something as trite as
the first breeze of spring or ramps or garlic scapes or the memory of the ruby necklace
was such cause for
jubilation
and there was so, so *much* of it
everywhere
vast
and minute
and without end.
And it's unbelievable to me.
Unbelievable.

(Looks about her, sees it all receding. Almost a whisper:)

Unbelievable.

*(She is staring out, solitary. A suspended moment.
A door slams. Something heavy drops. Tim enters, carrying a plastic grocery bag.)*

TIM: Hey.
JULIE: Be still my heart, it's the Second Coming!

TIM: Mom, you know, that kind of remark really sets a very difficult standard for me.

JULIE: Sweetie, no—yes—no but you're *here*!

FAYE: That was a very noisy entrance, Timmy.

TIM: Oh! I dropped my bag on the chair but the chair was / gone

FAYE: *That's* what's missing: those Queen Anne chairs!

TIM: They're not Queen / Anne, actually

JULIE: Yes, I'm having them / reupholstered

TIM: You can tell by the / legs

JEFF *(Alarmed)*: Reupholstered; *why?*

JULIE: That's what we do.

Remember, Faye, Rivka? In Forest Hills? She could barely breathe anymore but there were paint samples hanging / from the kitchen cabinets

FAYE: Yes! A million different whites. You would have needed an Inuit to choose among them

JEFF: How much does it cost to reupholster two chairs, just as a point of / interest

JULIE: I don't know for certain. Two or three thousand / but it's worth it, he does exquisite work

JEFF: Jesus

JULIE *(Enough of this, aglow with the wonder of Tim's presence)*: You're back.

You've come back.

TIM *(Brushes it off)*: Uh yeah. *(Thrusts out a bunch of frowsy deli carnations)* I got you these, Aunt Faye.

FAYE: Darling boy, thank you.

TIM *(Hands Jeff a brick of cheese)*: And this is for you. I hope you like it.

JEFF: It's . . . cheddar.

TIM: I thought for a second Monterey Jack but then you seemed, I don't know, cheddar. Merry um Christmas, fellow Jews.

JEFF: Thank you, Tim.

TIM: Oh.

JULIE: Do you see? He was just out buying presents. How lovely. You're lovely.

TIM *(Shies away from that)*: . . . Oh . . . No.

JULIE: But you *are*.

TIM *(Now ashamed)*: . . . No.

JULIE: Come here.

TIM: Why?

JULIE: *Come.*

(Reluctantly, he comes. He hasn't yet looked directly at her.)

Look at me.

(He looks vaguely toward her.)

Look at me.

(He looks more nearly at her. She adjusts his head so it's pointed directly at her face. His eyes are subtly downcast. She adjusts his head again so that he must look at her. He looks at her. He very slightly trembles. Controls it. He doesn't cry. Beat. He doesn't cry for a second time.)

TIM *(Constricted)*: Can—?
　　　Can I—?

JULIE: Darling!

TIM: What?

JULIE: I'm going to teach you to *cook* now.

TIM: But—

JULIE: You're going to finish the dinner with me—we haven't eaten yet! My, how hungry we must be!— You're going to finish it with me and write down everything you learn. The *skills* you'll have before this evening is out!

TIM: But

JULIE: We'll start with the salad—you'll be garde-manger— Oh what fun—what *fun* this all is!

(And she gets him to go with her. A moment.)

FAYE: "The memory of the ruby necklace."

She still thinks of it.

I had no idea it mattered to her.

JEFF: Three thousand dollars on chairs that nobody sits in. It's hopeless. There's no way to fix it.

FAYE: Stop being a lawyer.

JEFF: I'm *not* a—

oh I am.

I am a lawyer. *(He stares into his empty glass)*

And as a lawyer, I say it's hopeless.

FAYE: Maybe not.

JEFF: Do you have some sort of secret information?

FAYE: Maybe I do.

JEFF *(Mutters, really to himself)*: Yeah, well maybe I do, too.

FAYE: Do you *know* the story of the ruby necklace?

JEFF: I do not.

Does it apply to the present situation? Or at the very least will it kill time until we're fed?

FAYE: I'll tell you and you decide.

It's a good story for Christmas, it has red in it.

And a miracle.

By the time I finish, I expect there'll be snow.

JEFF: Go on

FAYE: My mother had a ruby necklace—ask me how.

JEFF: How?

FAYE: I have no idea.

Was she a sultan's mistress there in the Old Country?

JEFF: Was she?

FAYE: I have no idea.

Did she steal it?

Was the family wealthy once?

JEFF: Did she? Were they?

FAYE: I have no idea.

Or . . . just possibly . . . was this necklace . . . a piece of crap?

JEFF: Was it?

FAYE: Of *course* it was.

What would this little shtetl maiden be doing with actual rubies? It was junk.

Except in her mind where it was . . .

JEFF: Rubies?

FAYE: In*deed.*

And so it became the family treasure.

And it was coming to me.

The only living girl.

As my dowry?

Some other time?

"When, Rivka, when do I get the ruby necklace?"

"It'll come to you when it comes, my girl."

Okay.

My wedding, bupkis.

My daughter's birth—nothing.

"Am I waiting for you to die, Mameleh?"

So I bide.

JEFF: And when did you finally

FAYE: Wait!

There's a twist.

So.

Benny finds Julie.

This beautiful girl.

From the movies yet.

A German Jew.

Which to my Galician mother is just a shiksa with a problem.

Mama's going to the wedding, she's *not* going to the wedding; she approves, she reserves the right to create mischief.

It's a headache of a situation because truth to tell by the time this wedding was happening, her opinion was of no concern to anyone.

Still, it would have been nice if she came to the party not wearing black crepe.

So.

Finally she's subdued into a single attitude:

chronic weary acceptance.

"I *accept* your girl, Benny.

I *accept* this union.

I *accept* whatever fruit may come from

your loins."

And a party is held to celebrate all this lovely clenched

tolerance.

Glasses clink.

Mama welcomes the bride with a toast. And a present:

Here, darling girl, is a token of our embrace

. . . What?

JEFF: The crappy rubies.

FAYE: Excellent: You're a listener.

The crappy rubies.

And as she hangs the crappy rubies on the swansdown

neck, she stares at me with a smile like a jack-o'-lantern

So that I know that a barely acceptable stranger trumps

me in her esteem.

That when I threw in my lot with the hoi polloi who

knocked me up, I threw her away, too.

JEFF: . . . That's . . . awful.

FAYE: Wait there's a sequel!

Quarter-century later—Mama's dying in Mount Sinai.

By now her venom is diluted by dementia.

Flashes of clarity, the odd sentence time traveling from

an intact brain.

Christmas—

*Christ*mas mind you—

Benny goes to see her.

At my behest.

Because Benny and hospitals Benny and impairment

Benny and any human material in sub-Nietzschean condi-

tion are not compatible.

But he goes.

The two of them alone.

And there's a flare of brain function:
What is it?
It's Mameleh saying:
"Benny, give Faye the necklace."
And right then—
I swear to you I would not invent cornball crap like this—
she perishes

. . .

Making it up to me is her last unfinished business

. . .

I was
in those days
a little nutsy myself, the theory was menopause, I say Soul-Rot.
And I have *proof.*
Because Benny came home and told the story.
And Julie stood next to him.
And she handed me the necklace.
She was grinning from ear-to-ear—no one had ever been so happy for me.
And there was this lifting.
I got lighter and lighter and . . . and lighter . . .
JEFF: Something about this sounds familiar.
FAYE: Have I told you this before?
Old people boil down to a handful of fables.
JEFF: I know you haven't.
FAYE: *Anyway*
(and this is where it starts to apply:)
One day
a few years ago
my widow's portion having dwindled
(because Mort was less interested than he should have been in policies and other legalities, I was *fine* but not extravagantly fine),
on a whim, I take the ruby necklace to be appraised.

Expecting it will lead to a bidding war between Wool-
worth's and Kresge's

and what do you think?

JEFF: Not so crappy?

FAYE: You don't know the half of it.

Which circles back to my earlier question:

How did Rivka, Sweetheart of the Pale of Settlement,
get her hands on this . . .

rutilated . . . asterized treasure?

And was this the source of discord between her and
bitter sister Ruchel?

JEFF: And . . .

FAYE: I have no idea.

(Beat. A memory.)

JEFF: "A fucking string of phony rubies"?

FAYE: What?

JEFF: I don't know what that is.

No.

Must be from a movie.

Where is it now?

FAYE: I sold it.

JEFF: Oh!

FAYE: It had done its job as a symbol: It was time it became cash.

JEFF: How much did you

FAYE: Ho-*ho*!

JEFF: Which you invested.

FAYE: Brilliantly.

And *re*invested even *more* brilliantly

JEFF: Good for you.

FAYE: I have gifts. And this is how I happen to know that people do secretly funnel money into other people's accounts.

JEFF: Have you been paying the rent here?

FAYE: You may join me if you'd like.

It's a form of disrespect I think you'd enjoy.

(Jeff nods.)

JEFF: Thank you.

FAYE: She's lived her life in a ridiculous fashion.
But I'd like to see it follow through that way.

(Julie and Tim reenter with plates.)

JULIE: Tim has made his first vinaigrette.

FAYE: Wonderful!

JEFF *(Simultaneous with above)*: Congratulations.

FAYE: How'd it turn out?

JULIE: No matter, I made another. But I do see chefly possibilities in him, he has a fine hand for a whisk.
Oh isn't this great?
At long last: Dinner is served!

TIM *(Antsy)*: Okay, so I'm going now.

JULIE: *What?*

(Beat.)

TIM: I've gotta go.

JULIE: . . . You *can't.*

(Beat.)

TIM: The restaurant—

JULIE: No one believes that, Tim.

(Beat.)

TIM: I've
. . .
I've got to—

JULIE: You *can't.*
This is Christmas.

My . . . it's . . . there won't *be* . . .

It's *Christ*mas

TIM: We're, um, Jews?

JULIE: *No.*

I won't allow it.

You cannot break my heart twice in one evening.

It can't stand it, it's too compromised.

You are staying all evening and through the night.

You're sleeping here.

I don't care what I have to do to make you.

I'll pull out every stop, I'll say, "Is this the thanks a mother gets?" I'll hire a translator and say it in Yiddish but you cannot leave me.

(Beat.)

TIM: I've

gotta *go*

JULIE: Why?

(Beat.)

TIM: Molly

JULIE: *Mo*lly!

TIM *(A plea)*: Mom—?

JULIE: I demand that you stay.

I *demand* it.

(Beat.)

I know I have . . . made mistakes

TIM: But you haven't

JULIE: I know I have but please?

TIM: . . . I

JEFF: Tim, I have reached that point where I'm willing to break any promise I never made in the first place.

(Tim looks to Jeff. Beat.)

TIM: So like? Molly is . . . in a manner of speaking . . . pregnant?

(Consternation, exclamations from the women.)

JULIE *(Scolding)*: Did you not use a
TIM: No
JULIE: *Scotty?* And you didn't
TIM: Jeez this entire room is, like, obsessed with prophylaxis—
JULIE: I will not have two children succumb to
    this dread plague
TIM: No one is succumbing to this dread plague! . . . I'm not /
    succumbing
JULIE: I could *hit* you right now, Timothy; I could
    beat you up
TIM: I know.

(Beat. Julie tries to think what to ask.)

JULIE: Have you given any thought yet to
TIM: Of *course* I've thought about it, Mom
JULIE: Have you, have the *two* of you made any decisions?
TIM: . . . I can't say we've de*ci*ded anything.
JULIE: Have you *weighed*
TIM: We're not either of us decisive people. Persons.
    A person. Neither of us is *a*
JULIE: It's time that you become
JEFF: For Christ's sake, she's eight months pregnant!

(Beat.)

JULIE: Is this *true?* She's eight months pregnant?
TIM: Yup.
    Eight months.

(Beat.)

Nine, actually.
JEFF: Nine?
TIM: Yeah. I don't know why I *shaved off* that month.

(Everyone takes this in.)

He was born sixteen days ago.

(Lots of reactions.)

JEFF: Is *that* true?
TIM: Yeah, that one's true.
    And he's not a *girl* or anything like that. These are the
    facts.
JULIE: . . . So . . . where . . . what—
    Has he a *name*?
TIM: Well, he's a boy, so obviously we were gonna name him
    Scott so obviously . . . we did.
JULIE *(Soft)*: Oh . . . Thank you.
TIM: No problem.
JULIE: Well . . . where *is* he?
    Where *is* this child?
TIM: He's in Weehawken.
JULIE: Weehawken? / Oh, yes.
TIM: At my a*part*ment in
JULIE: And is he . . . warm . . .
    and do you *feed* him?
    You know you have to feed him, right?
TIM: Yeah, oh yeah, absolutely.
    He's
    on a *liquid* diet so far, he's . . .
    really cute.
    But I've gotta get back and spell Molly 'cause she gets
    tired.

> She had this baby sixteen days ago, which is *tiring*
> and we've got this great downstairs neighbor who helps
> out and is really great with Scotty but he does *way* too
> much crystal meth so

JULIE: Bring the baby here.

TIM: . . .

> I will

JULIE: Now.

TIM: Are you sure you're constitutionally capable of
> withstanding the

JULIE: *NOW!*

> *And* his mother.

TIM: How do I—

FAYE: *Get them.* We'll call a car service to meet you there.
> Bring the baby, bring the mother, bring the frankincense,
> bring the myrrh, just *go.*

TIM: Okay . . . okay.

> Okay—okay.
> *(To Julie)* Okay?

(She smiles at him. Nods.)

> Okay.

(He runs out.)

FAYE: Oy. That one.

(Julie collapses into a chair. They rush to her.)

JEFF: Are you all right?

JULIE: I am.

> Yes.
> I'm *strong.*

JEFF: Can I get you some water?

JULIE: No, no. I don't need it.

It's been a large night.

There's going to be a baby here

JEFF: It seems so.

JULIE: And I realize they turn into people and we all know how *that* goes but still . . .

it's hard not to . . .

do you know?

FAYE: Sure. Even Shelley—sorry.

JULIE: I'm a grandmother.

I got to be a grandmother! . . .

I haven't lost him . . .

FAYE: No.

JULIE: I don't know. I don't know . . . I'm racing, my mind is . . .

I've never believed in God and I'm certainly not going to start now.

But it's so hard to resist thinking that some things are portents, do you know? Symbols?

JEFF: Sure.

JULIE: You were wrong before, Faye, when you said, what a way to start a century. The century doesn't start for another week.

And last month's political atrocity—that was the final enormity of the last century, not the first of the new one and something about . . . the way things are working out . . .

It's making me believe that things are about to get so much better!

FAYE: Of course they are.

JULIE: And I don't mind missing it.

Just trusting it will happen is enough.

Jeff!

JEFF: Yes?

JULIE: You have tons of money.

JEFF: I—not—*tons*, I—sure . . .

JULIE: Buy this apartment.

JEFF: . . . Pardon?

JULIE: You've always *loved* this apartment.

JEFF *(Yes, but . . .)*: I *have.*

JULIE: Well, then!

JEFF: . . . But

yes, but

you don't *buy* things just because you love them.

JULIE: Don't you?

It makes so much sense.

After all you're going to be taking care of Timmy.

And his *fam*ily . . .

He's the loveliest boy ever to trod the earth but he's . . .

What's the word, Faye?

FAYE: Meshuggeh, or if that's overused, there's a host of others

JULIE: No. That will do.

Though I think he's going to be fine now. I really do.

I see the most dazzling life for him.

But he'll need some help bridging.

And of course that will be your responsibility, Jeff;

so you might as well all be under the same roof!

Don't you agree, Faye?

FAYE: Absolutely.

JULIE: And you'll come, too!

FAYE: Oh?

JULIE: You've used up Roslyn and you be*long* in the city

And there are so many rooms. You can fix them up! You can bring this place back.

And you can watch over Jeff as he watches over Timmy and Molly and Scotty—

Timmy and Molly and Scotty and Faye—it's like a cummings poem!—

Jeff! You said Scotty would be back tonight and you were right!

Prophet! You're a prophet unrecognized in—well, everywhere, really!

FAYE: You know, it's not an orthodox setup by my generation's way of thinking, but it makes sense. Times change.

JULIE: Yes, times change and new symmetries develop.

   It makes *so much* sense!

JEFF: But

JULIE: And you really haven't made any other arrangements, have you?

JEFF: . . . No.

JULIE: Oh—one fell swoop!

   I'm not going to push you for an answer.

   You can think about it while I get the salad.

   It will take me fifteen seconds.

(She exits.)

JEFF: This is crazy.

FAYE: Nu?

JEFF: I doubt I could afford it even if I

FAYE: Just say yes

JEFF: But

FAYE: It's not as if she's gonna know.

(Julie returns with salad.)

JEFF: Yes.

JULIE: Oh, lovely. *(She puts down the salad and hugs him)*

   Thank you.

   This is such a nice ending.

   Of course, I'm the only one who gets to end but it's very nice for me.

FAYE: I have to call the car service; what's the address of their manger?

JULIE: It's in my book on the escritoire.

FAYE: I'll get it. What a party you're going to have, my darling.

JULIE: Oh yes.

   What a beautiful Christmas this has turned out to be.

   The best ever.

Everything's so . . . promising. Isn't it?
So hopeful

(She looks out, sees it.)

Yes . . . yes.

(Hold.)

END OF PLAY

RICHARD GREENBERG is the author of *Three Days of Rain*, *Take Me Out*, *The American Plan*, *The Dazzle*, *The Violet Hour* and many other plays.